The
BOOK *of*
BLOOD

The BOOK of BLOOD

FROM LEGENDS AND LEECHES TO VAMPIRES AND VEINS

HP NEWQUIST

To Lee, Anne, Robert,
Edward, Margaret,
James, and Michael.

Apparently, blood really
is thicker than water.

Houghton Mifflin Books for Children is an imprint of Houghton
Mifflin Harcourt Publishing Company.

www.hmhbooks.com

The book design is by YAY! Design.
The text of this book is set in Goudy Old Style.
Photo credits are on page 149.

Library of Congress Cataloging-in-Publication Data
Newquist, H. P. (Harvey P.)
The book of blood : from legends and leeches to vampires and veins /
HP Newquist.
p. cm.
ISBN 978-0-547-31584-3
1. Blood—Juvenile literature. I. Title.
QP91.N45 2012
612.1'1—dc23
2011025134

Manufactured in China
SCP 10 9 8 7 6 5 4 3
4500444854

Contents

Introduction

RED. WET. STICKY. GROSS. MOST OF ALL, RED. BRIGHT RED.

All of these words are used to describe the most important liquid in your body: blood.

It's not just you, of course. Fish, birds, mammals, insects, and every person on the planet has blood, too.

Blood is pervasive. Blood—as a symbol, as a living tissue, even as a word—is important to every culture in the world. It is used in language to describe extreme situations or events. For example, "blood brothers" are people who have a very close relationship, while the phrase "bad blood between them" describes people who are spiteful toward each other. "Blue bloods" are members of a royal or very rich family who are thought to be different

The sight of blood from a wound causes many people to feel faint.

from common people—right down to the color of their blood. A "blood oath" is an oath that can never be broken. "Cold-blooded" refers to someone who appears to have no feelings or compassion. "Bloodthirsty" is used to describe the rulers of countries who regularly engage in war, with battles that might end up as "bloodbaths." Something that makes you extremely angry makes your "blood boil." And in England, "bloody" is used as a curse word.

Despite its importance to our lives, there has always been an "ick" factor surrounding blood. From vampires to scary movies, the thought of blood outside our bodies still gives most people the shivers. Bloodsucking vampires, blood transfusions in a hospital, and even the blood from a wound make many people queasy. They don't like to think that this red fluid fills up our insides.

Blood does give us a reason to pause, perhaps because of its bright red color. All over the world, red is the color of warning and danger. From stop signs and stoplights to fire engines and the flashing lights on ambulances, red is a color that we pay attention to. Similarly, the sight of blood causes us to freeze in our tracks.

There is more to blood than that it's red and kind of gross. It is an extremely complex fluid that moves through you your entire life without ever stopping. Most important, it keeps you alive. Blood delivers fresh oxygen to your cells, protects you from disease, and sweeps the waste from your organs from the moment you are born.

Scientists are still discovering things about blood almost every day. In fact, only in the last one hundred years have scientists come to understand just what blood is and what it does. And what it is, and does, is quite amazing.

CHAPTER 1

Real Blood

There is probably nothing scarier to many of us than seeing blood suddenly rush out of a wound. But without blood, people couldn't live. That red liquid is keeping you healthy, allowing you to think and play, and making sure your body gets everything it needs to grow and stay alive.

You've seen blood, probably coming out of your own body. This doesn't happen on purpose: You run into someone while playing a game, bang your face, and your nose starts bleeding. You open an envelope with your finger, get a paper cut, and then a razor-thin line of blood rises on your skin. You fall off your bike, and your scraped knee spills blood. You lose a tooth, and blood shows up in your mouth.

You see the blood, and you experience a moment of shock or fright that it has shown up outside your body. But the red liquid stops flowing, hardens, or is wiped off, and then you forget about it. It was there briefly, and then it went away.

There probably wasn't much blood, maybe a tablespoon at most. It was only a small amount of the blood that continued to swirl through your body, rushing as fast as if it were flowing through a faucet. You went back to what you were doing, and your blood kept doing what it has done ever since you were born: keeping you alive.

Blood looks too simple to be so important: just a bright red splash of liquid that seems as if it isn't much different from paint or fruit juice or cherry-colored water. But blood is not a simple red liquid. It is very complex and contains many components, which are so small you need a microscope to see them. Think of these components as being similar to the ingredients in a chocolate milk shake. While a glass of pure orange juice is made up only of the liquid squeezed from an orange, a chocolate milk shake is made up of many different things. There is the milk, sugar, and flavoring that create the ice cream. Then there is chocolate syrup, which has cocoa butter, sugar, corn syrup, preservatives, and a host of other ingredients. When blended together, these unrelated ingredients form one unique liquid: a milk shake.

Like a chocolate milk shake, a lot of things go into making your blood. This starts with plasma, a pale, gold-colored liquid that makes up half of your blood. Most of your plasma, about 90 percent, is made up of water. The watery nature of plasma helps blood flow through your body. Think of plasma as the river in which all the other blood parts float along together.

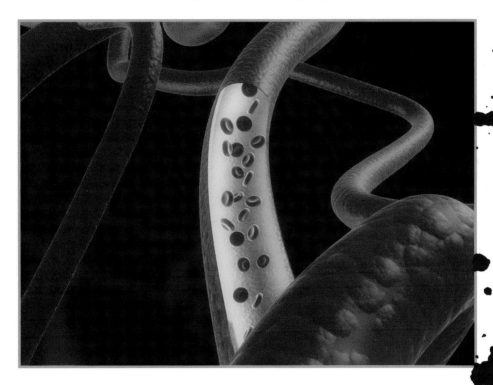

The next biggest ingredient in blood is red blood cells. These are round, partly flattened cells that carry hemoglobin. Hemoglobin is a protein, and proteins are substances that contain elements such as oxygen, nitrogen, and carbon. Living beings use proteins to carry nutrients and to trigger many biological processes. Hemoglobin, in particular, contains iron atoms that attract oxygen atoms. When red blood cells enter your lungs, the hemoglobin picks up oxygen and carries it to other parts of your body.

One drop of blood is mostly plasma, with red blood cells, white blood cells, and platelets floating inside it.

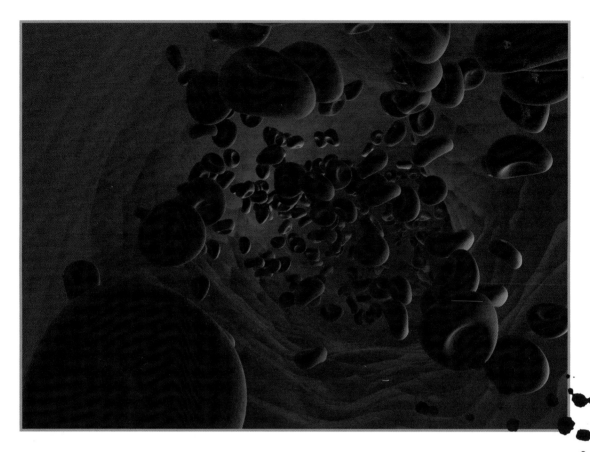

Hemoglobin turns bright red when it is filled with oxygen. And even though plasma is gold colored, nearly half of your blood is made up of red blood cells, so hemoglobin gives your blood its distinctive color.

Then we have white blood cells. There is approximately one white blood cell for every six hundred red blood cells—that's approximately 1 percent of your total blood—and they live for just a couple of weeks. Because there are so few of them, the white cells don't affect the color of your blood. (If there were as many white cells as there are red cells, we might be talking about pink blood.) White blood cells are like bodyguards for the inside of your body. They attack and eat bacteria, they eat dead cells in your body, they

Red blood cells are shaped like disks with slight depressions in their center. They get brighter red when they fill with fresh oxygen.

fight off parasites, and they tell your body when it needs to protect itself. Think of them as microscopic attack dogs. They also carry your DNA, which is the code to how your body is structured.

Aside from red and white blood cells, there are platelets, the smallest of the blood particles. Platelets are initially shaped like little plates, which makes it easy to remember their name, but when they go to work, they extend in many directions, like a star or a squid. The function of platelets is to stop blood from flowing out of you. When you get a cut or a scrape that starts to bleed, the platelets are suddenly exposed to air. They swell up and begin a chemical reaction that clogs up the blood flow near the cut. If you didn't have platelets, you would bleed to death.

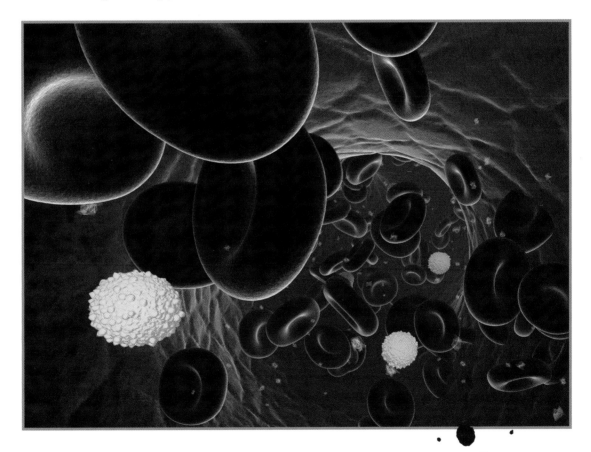

White blood cells are far outnumbered by red blood cells.

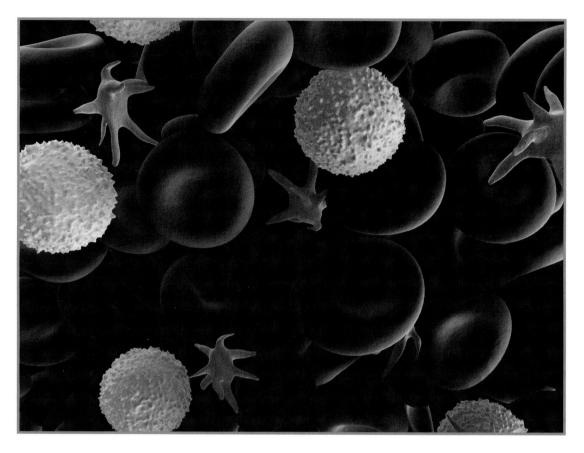

There are lots of other things in your blood, many of them floating around in the plasma. They include various proteins, vitamins, and glucose (a form of sugar), all of which are used to either nourish your body or help it fight off disease.

Your blood is a fluid rich with different-colored ingredients that do many things: golden plasma that transports blood cells, red blood cells with hemoglobin, white blood cells for protection, and platelets for clotting and repair. Inside your body there is about a gallon of this blood, the equivalent of a big jug of milk.

Because it contains living cells, blood is more than just a liquid. It is actually considered tissue. The definition of "tissue" is any grouping of cells that work together to perform a specific

**Platelets help keep your blood inside your body
when you are injured.**

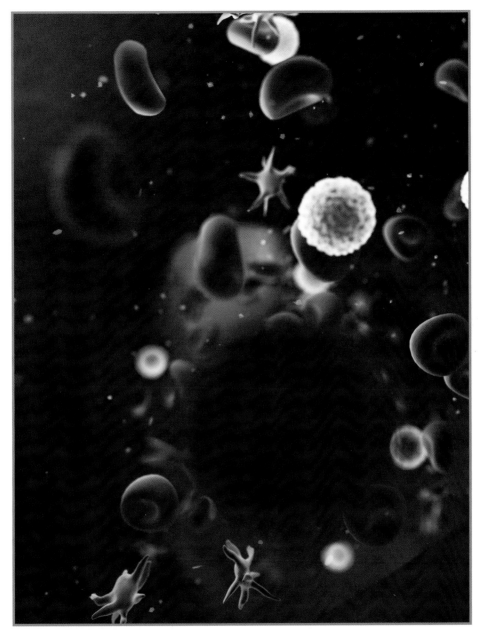

function or create a specific organ or part of the body. The heart and lungs and skin are all made of different forms of tissue. In the scientific world, blood is its own kind of tissue, even though it is a very fluid substance.

Red blood cells, white blood cells, platelets, and plasma are the primary components of blood.

BREAKDOWN OF BLOOD COMPONENTS IN A CENTRIFUGE

When blood is spun around quickly in a centrifuge, it separates into its three main parts based on how heavy each component is. The top half, or roughly 55 percent, of the separated blood is the almost clear gold-colored plasma. The bottom segment, just 45 percent, is made up of all the heavy elements related to red blood cells and hemoglobin. In the middle is a small layer—barely 1 percent—of white blood cells and platelets. They are slightly heavier than plasma, but lighter than red blood cells. This is called the buffy coat because of its off-white or buff color.

Blood moves around your body through a vast network called the cardiovascular system. This includes your heart, your arteries, your veins, and your capillaries (the really tiny blood vessels). Various scientists refer to this network as the circulatory

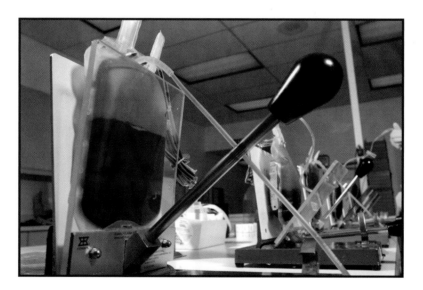

Blood separates into its different parts when it is processed in a lab: red blood (on the bottom), white blood (thin strip in the middle), and plasma (on the top).

system. Others use the term "circulatory system" to mean both the cardiovascular system and the lymphatic system, which is part of the immune system and helps drain excess fluids from your organs. To keep it simple, we're going to use the term "circulatory system" from here on. It's the most commonly used term, and will help

BLUE BLOOD?

While it is in your body, your blood is always red. It is never blue, although some people think that blood is blue because some veins look blue underneath our skin. The fact is that oxygen-rich blood is bright red, and when red blood cells give up oxygen—and instead carry waste from your body—they lose that brightness. Blood turns dark red as it travels through you, becoming almost maroon or burgundy colored, before lightening again when it absorbs air in the lungs. The idea that blood is blue in your body is a myth.

In fact, your veins aren't blue, either. Veins appear blue under your skin because of the way light interacts with various layers of your skin, with the area around your veins taking on a darker color. And when you see blood vessels next to other parts of your skin, you perceive them as bluish in color.

you better understand how blood moves—in a circular manner—throughout the body.

Think of the circulatory system as a highway or a waterway. Blood flows through it like traffic, carrying everything your body needs, as well as most of what your body wants to get rid of. Like a busy highway in a big city, traffic never stops: it crisscrosses over itself and loops around and up and over, and eventually everything gets to its proper destination.

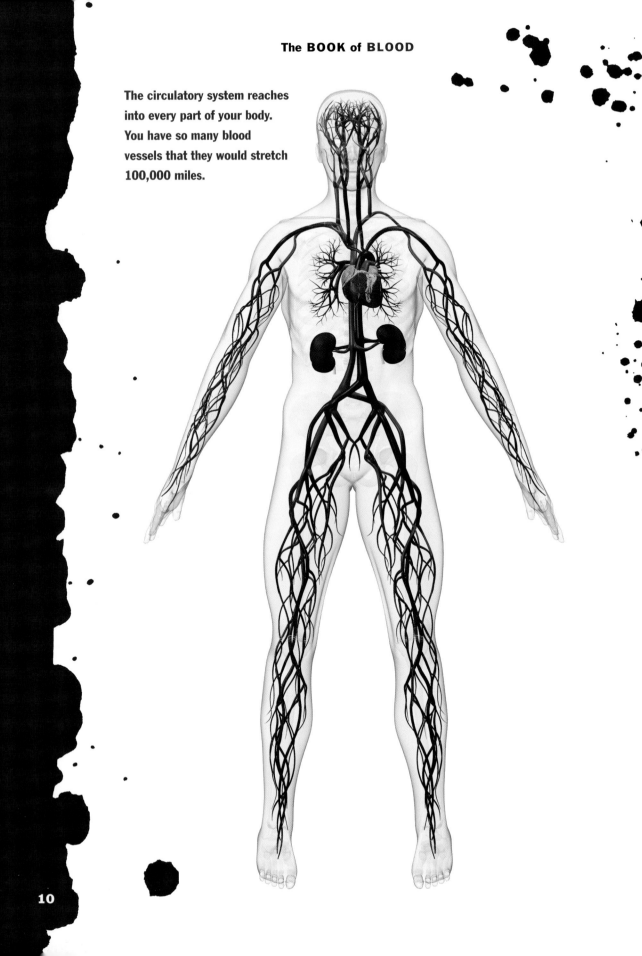

The circulatory system reaches into every part of your body. You have so many blood vessels that they would stretch 100,000 miles.

The circulatory system is so completely spread out over the human body that if you poke a needle into any part of your skin, you will draw blood. This is because there are approximately a hundred thousand miles of veins, arteries, and capillaries in your body. If all of these blood vessels were stretched out in a line, they would circle the Earth four times. You can see capillaries—large ones—by looking at your eyeball in the mirror or by looking up close at a friend's eye. Those little red vessels in the white part of your eyeball are carrying blood right into your eye from your heart.

Each day, your heart beats about a hundred thousand times, pumping blood to every single corner of your body. Your heart pumps your blood over and over so many times over the course of twenty-four hours that it is pumping the equivalent of two thousand gallons a day. Two thousand gallons is enough to fill a swimming pool.

Unlike with many other systems in your body, you can actually see and feel the circulatory system at work. You can feel your heart pumping, you can sometimes see your arteries pulsing (especially in your wrists and arms), and you've seen blood come out of your body, probably through cuts, loose teeth, or a bloody nose.

That brings us to the big question: what does blood actually do?

We're fortunate to be living in an age when we can answer that question. Before the 1900s, there were a lot of misconceptions about blood. It was misunderstood and frightening, part of monster stories and mythology. And not so long ago, doctors believed that curing diseases meant injecting animal blood into people . . . or taking as much blood out of a person as they could.

To find out what blood does, we'll start by looking at why blood has always been so mysterious.

CHAPTER 2

The Mystery Inside

reatures have bled since the dawn of time. Dinosaurs bled, mammoths bled, and the Neanderthals (sometimes referred to as cavemen) bled.

Modern humans, who have been around for a little over two hundred thousand years, saw blood regularly. It poured from the animals they hunted. It flowed from their own bodies when they were injured. This might have happened when they fell or when animals attacked them. A savage animal attack—by a predator such as a lion— would have been very dramatic and involved a great deal of blood.

After a predator had finished eating another animal, the only thing left may have been blood on the dirt.

Early humans had no understanding of what blood was or what it did, but they understood that it was important. They knew that when a lot of blood was spilled on the ground, death was nearby. By being associated with death, blood was certain to have caused fear. It was given the same respect as death.

Like other powerful images, symbols, and elements of the natural world that weren't understood (such as thunder, lightning, floods, predatory animals, and death), blood was incorporated into the lives of ancient cultures. It became part of their legends, part of their rituals, and part of their ceremonies. Blood was essential to myths, legends, and religious traditions long before humans knew what blood was.

As far back as 5000 B.C., the people of Mesopotamia (the area of present-day Iraq) had a female goddess known as Lamashtu. She was an evil creature who was jealous of human women, stole their babies, and sucked the blood from

Lamashtu attacked citizens and drank their blood. In this ancient plaque, she is depicted devouring the people around her.

the mothers and their newborns. Her existence was used to explain the deaths of infants and of pregnant women. Other evil, blood-drinking beings, like the Babylonian goddess Lilitu and the Hebrew Lilith, are believed to be related to the story of Lamashtu.

The Hindu goddess Kali, who was associated with change and destruction, was said to drink the blood of her enemies after defeating them on the battlefield. Sekhmet, the warrior goddess of Egypt, also drank the blood of her enemies and was said to drink from the Nile River when the water became bloody. It is likely that some of these female deities were the inspiration for early vampire legends.

Kali and Sekhmet were ancient deities who were believed to drink blood.

Blood also played a large part in the Bible, and it was used frequently as a symbol of fear, power, and life—especially when God was involved. In the Old Testament book of Exodus, the Egyptians held the Israelites as slaves. When God demanded that the Israelites be freed, the Egyptians refused. As punishment, God unleashed ten plagues upon Egypt, beginning with the Plague of Blood:

> *Thus says the LORD, "By this you shall know that I am the LORD: behold, I will strike the water that is in the Nile with the staff that is in my hand, and it will be turned to blood. The fish that are in the Nile will die, and the Nile will become foul, and the Egyptians will not be able to drink its water.*
>
> *Exodus 7:17–18*

A picture of the Nile River "turning to blood," killing all the fish. (From the 1300s, artist unknown, British Library)

Scientists think that the "river of blood" identified in the Bible and in the legends of Sekhmet may have been caused by the red ash of a volcano or by the spread of algae that is red in color. The Nile also takes on a reddish color when it floods and red soil seeps into it.

Rivers running with blood are pretty horrific. Yet, this plague didn't persuade the Egyptians to free the slaves, nor did the next eight plagues, which included frogs, lice, locusts, and darkness. But the tenth plague did change the Egyptians' minds, and it too involved blood. For the tenth plague, God sent an angel to kill all the firstborn male children in Egypt. However, God warned the Israelites ahead of time to mark their doors with lambs' blood. This would be a sign to the angel not to harm the children inside.

After all this blood, the Egyptians gave up and let the Israelites go.

Later in the Old Testament, the book of Leviticus states that blood is to be used only as part of sacrifices to God. It is to be sprinkled on altars, but no one is ever to drink it. Modern researchers think this might be a reference to other cultures of the time—primarily in North Africa and in Egypt—where people drank blood for medicinal purposes.

The biblical importance of blood extends into the New Testament, where Jesus Christ tells his disciples during the Last Supper that the meal is representative of his life. In Mark 14:23–24 the Bible says: "And he took the cup, and when he had given thanks, he gave it to them: and they all drank of it. And he said unto them, This is my blood of the new testament, which is shed for many."

In John 19:34, as Christ is on the cross, a soldier stabs him in his side with a spear. According to the Bible, both blood and water flowed from the wound. This is interpreted to represent death, in the form of blood, and new life and purity, in the form of water.

BLOOD SACRIFICE

The reverence for blood appears to have extended to almost all ancient religions, cultures, and civilizations. Its mentions in the Old Testament date from two thousand years ago. The Chinese legend of P'an ku, the creature whose blood formed the Earth's rivers, is over three thousand years old. The importance of blood in

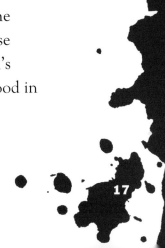

ancient Egyptian mythology dates from nearly six thousand years ago.

Over the course of thousands of years, blood took on a prominent role as an offering to gods. After all, if blood was part of death, and the gods were responsible for life and death, then these gods must like blood. Perhaps giving them blood more often would keep them happy and make them look more favorably on their worshipers.

This belief cropped up in civilizations around the world. Almost every ancient culture created some sort of blood sacrifice as part of its rituals for its gods. The Hebrews used the blood of lambs to protect them from an avenging angel. Ancient Romans spilled the blood of cattle to purify their towns and drive away evil spirits. Warrior kings during the Shang dynasty in China offered the blood of their people to their dead ancestors in the hope of being victorious in war.

Lambs' blood was used as protection in Old Testament stories, as depicted in this stained glass window.

Ancient paintings from Greece and pottery from Mayan civilizations—two cultures that existed on separate continents—depict ritual bloodletting, a process whereby blood was taken from an animal or a human as part of a ritual or ceremony.

In these ceremonies, the human being who was being sacrificed for his or her blood usually died, since it required that throats be cut, stomachs opened up, or heads removed. Taking blood for ceremonies was not a pretty sight. It involved quite a bit of struggling and screaming. And lots of blood.

Ritual bloodletting—which is different from medical bloodletting, a procedure we'll explore in later chapters—was practiced by civilizations such as the ancient Egyptians and Mayans. It was performed by a priest or tribal chief who took the spilling blood from the severed throat or stomach of the victim. The blood was collected in a special bowl, and then sprinkled over an altar or over members of the tribe to bless them. Some priests actually drank it.

A special knife used for cutting open sacrificial victims.

Many of these rituals had very strict rules and could be carried out only by prominent members of the tribe—those considered worthy enough, powerful enough, or wise enough to take a life. Performing the rituals often involved the gathering of the entire tribe, who would watch the action. Like today's religious ceremonies, these were very serious occasions, and sacred objects would be used to carry out the ritual. These included finely carved blades used only for drawing blood and bowls fashioned from the tops of skulls to collect the flowing blood.

Sometimes the human sacrifice was a person from a neighboring tribe who had been captured in battle or kidnapped for the event. These people must have been horrified at the thought of being killed in an enemy's ritual. At other times, the sacrifice was someone from within the tribe who willingly offered him- or herself up. That person might have felt honored to be chosen by the tribe as a gift to the gods. The most important thing, as far as the tribe was concerned, was that these victims were giving their lives for the benefit of many others.

Blood rituals occurred all over the world. Mayan kings and queens, who ruled in Central America from nearly 2000 B.C. to A.D. 1500, would cut open their own veins so that their blood could be used during ceremonies. The Greek leader Alexander the Great (356–323 B.C.), ruler of Macedonia, was said to have started each day by sacrificing an animal with a knife and then praying to the gods over the animal's blood.

Perhaps no society was as fond of spilling blood as the Aztecs. In the late 1400s in what is now Mexico, the Aztecs took blood sacrifice to a new level. They built pyramid temples that had altars on top. Sacrificial humans were taken up to the altars on eighteen festivals during the year to celebrate everything from the oldest

members of the community to crop harvests.

Once those to be sacrificed were on the altars, their hearts were cut out and their blood was allowed to flow down over the temple steps. The Aztecs were thought to have killed thousands of people in this way every year. They believed it was important to honor the gods with this blood because the gods had sacrificed much to create the universe. The Aztecs were just paying the gods back.

One of the unusual things about all this bloodletting is that very few cultures learned much about how the human body worked from all of the slicing and cutting that was done on sacrifices. In fact, it was considered immoral and illegal to cut open a body,

An image from a sixteenth-century Spanish document showing the Aztecs performing a human sacrifice on a pyramid.

alive or dead, unless this was done for purely religious purposes. The Aztecs, for instance, took the heart out of the chest of their sacrifice, but they immediately disposed of the body. They did not worry about all the parts that the heart was connected to. The body was sacred (even when it belonged to an unwilling victim) and was not to be touched for any purpose other than making the gods happy.

Only the Egyptians, who turned their rulers into mummies after death, were interested in what was going on in the human body. Their method of creating mummies relied upon extracting organs through tiny slits made in the skin. They wanted to preserve bodies for this trip to the afterlife (the Egyptian version of heaven and hell), so they didn't open people up and look inside. People

Making dead people into mummies was a way of preparing those people for the afterlife.

needed their bodies in the afterlife, and cutting up their flesh would have disfigured them.

Organs were removed so that bodies could be treated with herbs and oils, and then stuffed with dry cloth. The heart, lungs, kidneys, and other organs were placed in sealed jars to preserve them separately. By removing these organs through surgical slits, the Egyptians became familiar with the placement of organs and the movement of fluids through the body.

Even doctors in Greece and Rome, where the great classical philosophers lived, did not examine bodies after death. It was considered inappropriate and disrespectful of the dead person. Because of this ban, doctors had little sense of how things worked inside the human body. Most of them thought that blood just floated under the skin like water in a jar.

THE FOUR HUMORS

The first ideas about what blood might actually do came from Hippocrates, a physician and teacher who lived in Greece from 460 to 377 B.C. Little is known of Hippocrates' personal life, but he wrote extensively about the way doctors should treat their patients. Prior to his teachings, doctors were as likely to trust in magic as they were to give treatments that would help sick patients.

Hippocrates taught that doctors needed to do everything they could to heal a patient, and that they needed to always act with the patient's health in mind. This included never knowingly doing harm, prescribing deadly drugs, and performing surgery that they were not trained for. So important were Hippocrates' ideas that even today doctors take what is called the Hippocratic oath, a promise to treat their patients as best as they can.

HIPPOCRATIC OATH

swear by Apollo the Physician and Asclepius and Hygieia and Panaceia and all the gods, and goddesses, making them my witnesses, that I will fulfill according to my ability and judgment this oath and this covenant:

To hold him who has taught me this art as equal to my parents and to live my life in partnership with him, and if he is in need of money to give him a share of mine, and to regard his offspring as equal to my brothers in male lineage and to teach them this art—if they desire to learn it—without fee and covenant; to give a share of precepts and oral instruction and all the other learning to my sons and to the sons of him who has instructed me and to pupils who have signed the covenant and have taken the oath according to medical law, but to no one else.

I will apply dietetic measures for the benefit of the sick according to my ability and judgment; I will keep them from harm and injustice.

I will neither give a deadly drug to anybody if asked for it, nor will I make a suggestion to this effect. Similarly I will not give to a woman an abortive remedy. In purity and holiness I will guard my life and my art.

I will not use the knife, not even on sufferers from stone, but will withdraw in favor of such men as are engaged in this work.

Whatever houses I may visit, I will come for the benefit of the sick, remaining free of all intentional injustice, of all mischief and in particular of sexual relations with both female and male persons, be they free or slaves.

What I may see or hear in the course of treatment or even outside of the treatment in regard to the life of men, which on no account one must spread abroad, I will keep myself holding such things shameful to be spoken about.

If I fulfill this oath and do not violate it, may it be granted to me to enjoy life and art, being honoured with fame among all men for all time to come; if I transgress it and swear falsely, may the opposite of all this be my lot.

Hippocrates, like many doctors before him, thought that blood was just one of four important liquids in the body. These were called the four humors and included blood, phlegm, yellow bile, and black bile. (The word "humors" doesn't have anything to do with being funny, although it sounds that way. Once upon a time "humors" referred to liquids.) This belief in four humors tied in with the Greek view that nature was made up of four primary elements: fire, water, earth, and air. There was even a relationship between the four humors and the four elements. The essence of fire was thought to be part of yellow bile, earth was supposed to be contained in black bile, water was a component of phlegm, and all four elements—including air—were considered components of blood.

Each of the humors—or body fluids—controlled the body and kept it healthy. Too much of one fluid would cause particular kinds of sickness and disease. The body needed to keep the humors in perfect balance in order for people to be both healthy and happy.

The humors were defined like this:

Blood controlled general health and well-being. Too much blood caused fevers or ailments in the body.

Phlegm (mucus and saliva) controlled the body's activity level. Too much phlegm, and a person became sleepy or lazy.

Black bile controlled emotions. Too much of it made a person sad, depressed, or irritable.

A drawing of Hippocrates, one of the world's first great doctors.

25

Yellow bile controlled a person's temper. Too much of it made him or her angry, excitable, or out of control.

Even though real bile is a form of stomach acid, it's possible that the Greeks based their notions of bile on different blood forms: black bile could have been the dark form that clotted blood takes, and yellow bile could have been the light gold of blood plasma. Hippocrates might have seen these colors when blood stored in a container separated over time into its various parts (the way that salad dressing or fruit smoothies separate into different levels of liquid when they have been sitting around for a while).

When treating patients who were thought to have too much of one humor or another—depending on their symptoms—doctors such as Hippocrates tried removing some of the humors. This was done by making the patient throw up, by giving the patient a medicine that would cause diarrhea, or by draining specific amounts of blood from the body. It was not very scientific by today's standards, but it was very popular two thousand years ago.

Illustrations of the differences in the four humors from the seventeenth century.

Actually, it was popular until about two hundred years ago.

Hippocrates' extensive study of patients led him to create a guide to adjusting the level of blood in a patient. He had a precise bloodletting procedure where he would cut into a patient's vein and let a certain amount of blood flow out. Sometimes this was a substantial amount—almost enough to kill a person. This didn't stop the doctors. They believed that the weakness the patient was feeling from blood loss was a sign that the bad humor level was being brought back to normal.

Bloodletting as a medical practice had been around since before Hippocrates was born, but no one is quite sure who first undertook the procedure or why. By the time Hippocrates got around to doing it, bloodletting was a common medical occurrence. Hippocrates, though, was better able than his predecessors to outline the most effective ways to perform it.

Hippocrates didn't get to cut into patients to find out if there really was too much of one humor or another. Like other doctors

MELANCHOLLY.

THE FOWRE COMPLEXIONS.
SANGVINE.

in ancient times, he wasn't allowed to because of the laws that protected the bodies of the dead. Thus, most of his writings were based on observations of how people behaved when they were sick or injured. This wasn't a perfect way to learn about the body, but he had no choice. Yet, roughly seventy years after Hippocrates died, another Greek doctor found a way around the laws that prevented the internal examination of bodies.

GETTING INSIDE

Herophilus, a Greek doctor born in 335 B.C., was able to study the insides of humans by going to work in Alexandria, Egypt— across the Mediterranean Sea. Because there were no Egyptian laws at that time preventing the study of dead people, the rulers of Egypt allowed Herophilus to dissect dead bodies (called cadavers or corpses). These bodies were usually those of criminals, which made it somewhat easier for people to tolerate the idea of medical experiments on corpses.

In his studies, Herophilus examined the size, shape, color, hardness, softness, and function of internal organs. He also made detailed observations of how the human body's insides fit together—what went where and what was connected to what. He found out that veins and arteries were different—arteries were thicker than veins, but they both carried blood. His research was so extensive, and so original, that he is still known as the father of anatomy.

Herophilus was one of the only surgeons of his time allowed to see the insides of human bodies. There were other doctors who wanted to learn more about how human anatomy worked. The most creative of these was Claudius Galen of Pergamon, who lived around A.D. 150 in what is now modern-day Turkey. Even though he was a surgeon, Galen wasn't allowed to experiment on living humans. His job was to fix bodies that were already damaged. However, he had an interesting job that gave him access to the inside of humans: he was in charge of operating on gladiators who were injured in battles. Many gladiators suffered severe injuries, and Galen was able to look at their insides while he tried to patch them up.

When he wasn't working on gladiators, Galen cut open pigs and apes to see if their insides were like ours. He saw, as Herophilus had, that a system of veins and arteries carried blood around the bodies of mammals. But he thought that this network moved two types of blood. One type was the bright red blood carried by the arteries. This blood was full of oxygen, although Galen didn't know that. The other type was dark blood, almost maroon in color, and it was full of the dead cells and waste that the body needed to dispose of. Again, Galen didn't know this. As far as he could tell, there were two different kinds of blood, one changing into the other as it passed through "invisible" parts of the heart. Like Hippocrates, Galen thought that

Gladiators engaging in combat.

people could be cured of their illnesses by bloodletting.

Galen's research explored so much of the body that doctors and medical scientists used his ideas for more than a thousand years. That created a problem because very few people tried to improve on his studies and learn more about blood in the centuries after Galen's death. Thus, doctors practiced medicine using all the right ideas Galen had alongside the wrong ones, such as the two different kinds of blood.

It would be another thousand years before someone figured out that blood was the most important fluid in the body, and that the heart, lungs, and all the other organs needed blood to survive.

CHAPTER 3

Making Progress

E gypt was one of the most advanced civilizations, if not the most advanced, of the ancient world. Even as far back as 3100 B.C., Egypt's accomplishments were the envy of other nations. From designing pyramids and allowing medical experiments to building libraries and making mummies, the Egyptians demonstrated that they were technologically and intellectually far ahead of most of the world.

This was especially true when it came to learning about the human body. Egyptians had allowed Herophilus to come from Greece and open up the cadavers of nonroyal citizens in order to learn about anatomy. Egypt eventually produced its own scientists and doctors, whose skill rivaled those in Europe. It was an Egyptian doctor who figured out how blood flowed inside humans.

Ala al-Din Abu al-Hassan Ali ibn Abi-Hazm al-Qurashi al-Dimashqi, known simply as Ibn al-Nafis, lived in the thirteenth century in Cairo. He was born in Syria and went to Egypt—like others before him—to practice medicine. He became a great physician and wrote numerous books about medicine. Unlike Hippocrates or Galen, he realized that blood traveled inside a single network, the circulatory system. Ibn al-Nafis found that the heart was the central organ in this system and that it was the pump that kept blood moving throughout the body.

His most important discovery was that blood flowed from the heart to the lungs and back again. This was the first time that anyone had confirmed there was a direct connection between the dark blood from the veins and the bright blood from the arteries. It was all the same blood, but it changed as it passed through the heart and lungs and was exposed to air.

When not studying human anatomy, Ibn al-Nafis wrote books—lots of them. He wrote eighty books on medicine alone, but he also wrote about the Islamic religion, law, philosophy, proper diet, and even a novel known as *The Kamiliyah Treatise*, a work that many consider the world's first science fiction novel.

Unfortunately, the Egyptian empire and its accomplishments all but disappeared after it fell under Roman rule. European culture and thinking came to dominate Egypt, in part because Europeans viewed the Egyptians as idol-worshiping inferiors. Over the course

of hundreds of years, less and less importance was given to study and research performed by native Egyptians. Thus, Ibn al-Nafis's work was little known outside of Arab countries. Only centuries later did the rest of the world realize the groundbreaking nature of his work.

This was unfortunate, because it took another three hundred years for the Europeans to discover the relationship between the lungs and the heart for themselves. Even then, it remained a secret to most of Europe because of the way in which the discovery was revealed.

Europe was in turmoil during this time. The period from about the fifth century to the twelfth century was called the Dark Ages—for a very good reason. Entire countries had been destroyed by wars, diseases, and famine. Many regions of Europe had no laws or governments. Schools disappeared. The study of medicine and science all but dried up.

To make matters worse, various forms of the plague—a disease

The Egyptians built a thriving culture based on education and experimentation before becoming isolated from the rest of the world.

that can infect the bloodstream and the lungs—showed up regularly during the Dark Ages. Plagues were a problem not only during this time; they continued ravaging people until modern times. During the 1300s, one instance of a plague called the Black Death killed twenty-five million people in Europe. That was about one-third of the entire European population. The plague did even more damage in Asia, where, it has been estimated, as many as fifty million people died.

Every form of the plague (there are three) is deadly. One of its symptoms is bleeding from the mouth—not a natural occurrence. As the plague spread, people avoided those who had bloody mouths. A superstition arose that those with blood in their mouths were vampires, drinking the blood of the healthy to try to save themselves.

Since people in Europe had little or no education, they readily believed such superstitions. This period gave rise to ideas about witches and warlocks, as well as werewolves and vampires. There were no scientists—and no books or newspapers—in Europe to inform people otherwise. People would believe almost anyone who had a good explanation for what was going on around them— whether it was true or not.

Into this confusion came the strangest doctors to ever practice medicine: barbers. Yes, barbers, the people best known for cutting hair. During the Dark Ages and beyond, many barbers learned how to be surgeons. This happened because of two simple facts. The first was that many real surgeons died during plagues because they had been infected by the people they treated. The second was that barbers knew how to use razors, which was an important skill when you had to cut someone open. The lack of doctors and the ability to handle a very sharp knife gave barbers the opportunity to "play doctor" for real.

The easiest medical procedure for these barbers to perform was bloodletting, which around this time was given a serious, scientific-sounding name—phlebotomy. It became one of the most common forms of treating sickness all over Europe. Phlebotomy was thought to cure everything from colds and allergies to stomachaches and chicken pox.

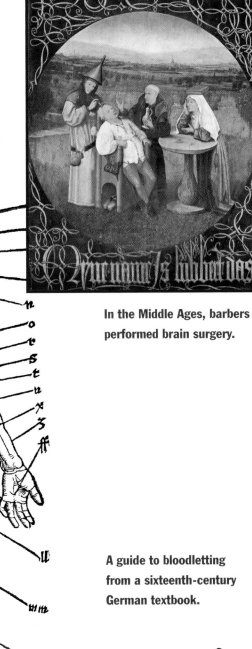

In the Middle Ages, barbers performed brain surgery.

A guide to bloodletting from a sixteenth-century German textbook.

Even after doctors took back medicine from the barbers around the 1400s, bloodletting continued. Good doctors prided themselves on their ability to take blood well enough that they didn't have to cut up their patients too badly. To aid them in this procedure were special tools called lancets. Lancets were like scalpels, and extremely sharp. They were developed to poke small holes in the skin, usually in the arm or leg. Doctors had to be

An image of a Frenchwoman undergoing bloodletting.

careful to hit a vein properly so as to open it up but not cut it in half. When the patient started bleeding, the blood was drained into a measuring cup so that the doctor could tell how much blood was being taken. Many doctors drained several pints of blood at a time, not realizing that the body needs about eight pints to function properly. Fainting from blood loss was a common side effect.

Lancets were so important to the medical profession that when one of the first medical journals was founded, in 1823, it was named *The Lancet*. It is still published to this day and is considered one of the most important medical publications in the world.

Other devices were created to help doctors make the proper cuts. These included spring-loaded lancets that would punch a hole in a vein with the press of a button. Another machine, called a scarificator, had a set of adjustable metal blades set into a box that would quickly cut a patient's skin to different depths to begin the bleeding.

Finally, there were leeches. These creatures, which are found all over the world, live on human blood (we'll see why in a later chapter). In cases where a doctor decided that a patient wasn't suitable to be "cut" or if there was a problem in a delicate place—especially around the face and head—leeches were used to suck the blood out of the patient. When the leech was full of blood, it was pulled off and another one put in its place.

It all sounds like the making of a modern-day horror movie,

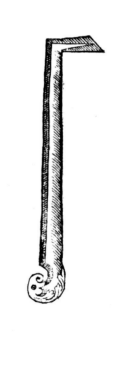

Illustration of lancets for making different-size cuts to draw blood.

but this was what scientists of the day considered the best medical treatment available.

The problem was that bloodletting didn't work. Bloodletting does not cure anything, and it never has. The best explanation for its popularity is that patients got weak from blood loss and would sleep for long periods to recuperate. Sleep is one of the best ways to treat common illnesses like the cold and flu because it gives the body a chance to focus all its resources on fighting the illness. When patients recovered after sleeping, passing out, or fainting, they frequently felt better. Doctors claimed this miraculous recovery was due to the bloodletting, not to much needed rest.

Doctors would not question the value of bloodletting until it killed George Washington, the first president of the United States, in 1799. But that was several hundred years into the future.

Out of the Dark

As the dismal days of the Dark Ages faded, schools reopened. Governments were established. Scientists and philosophers once again took to learning as much as they could about the world around them.

Names such as Copernicus, da Vinci, and Galileo would become famous from the sixteenth century on. But one man did not become quite so famous, even though he was the first European to

Leeches were used for bloodletting.

identify how blood flowed in the body. His name was Michael Servetus, and he was born in Spain in 1509. Although he was a very good scientist, his main interest was religion, especially the Protestant religions, which he didn't like very much.

Servetus also had a strong interest in medicine and studied the works of Galen while attending school in France. He decided that Galen had been wrong about the circulatory system and humans' having two types of blood. Servetus determined that blood changed from dark to light because of the way it moved from the heart to the lungs. Ibn al-Nafis had already figured this out three centuries earlier, but no one in Europe, including Servetus, knew it at the time.

An indication of Servetus's greater interest in religion than in medicine was that he didn't publish his findings on blood in a standard medical paper. Instead, he included his ideas as part of a paper he wrote that detailed what he thought was wrong with religions that had started up after the Protestant Reformation in 1517. His breakthrough on blood was literally buried deep within his religious writings.

He followed this paper with an anti-Protestant book that angered many church leaders, especially John Calvin, the head of a Protestant group in Switzerland. These leaders condemned him as a heretic, or nonbeliever, and threatened his life. Fearing for his safety, Servetus fled from France and, for some reason, went to Geneva, which happened to be where Calvin lived. When Calvin found out Servetus was in town, he had him arrested and imprisoned. Then he had Servetus burned at the stake, with the last copy of his book chained to his leg. The book, along with Servetus, was consumed by the fire.

Once again, knowledge of blood remained a secret because few doctors or scientists read Servetus's paper, thinking it contained only comments about religion. The next time someone figured out how blood flowed, it would have to be from scratch.

The man who finally brought the study of blood and the circulatory system out into the open for all to see was an extraordinary British surgeon named William Harvey. He was born in 1578 and was given a scholarship to medical school at the age of sixteen. He traveled all over Europe, studying at different universities, and was exposed to a wide variety of medical beliefs and procedures.

Servetus's writings on blood were eventually burned with him, as this image shows in the background.

By the time Harvey became a doctor, many governments had begun to allow some basic study of human anatomy through dissection—the cutting up of body parts to study their internal structure. Like the Egyptians many years before, government tended to restrict this study to the corpses of criminals. For example, England had very specific laws that permitted medical study only on the bodies of convicted murderers who had been executed. This meant that few bodies were available for study, and medical schools sometimes paid grave robbers to bring them fresh corpses so that surgeons could be trained before they operated on live patients. (It wasn't until a law was passed in 1832 that medical professionals were allowed to legally use donated bodies for research and study.)

In 1628 Harvey wrote a book about his medical research that changed medicine forever. He had performed experiments on a number of people, many involving the veins in the arms, and also explored the insides of animals. One of his experiments was very simple: he would tie a tight bandage around a patient's upper arm. This restricted the blood flow into the forearm, making it a little bit cooler than the rest of the body. When he untied the bandage, the vessels would swell, and he could see the veins in the forearm

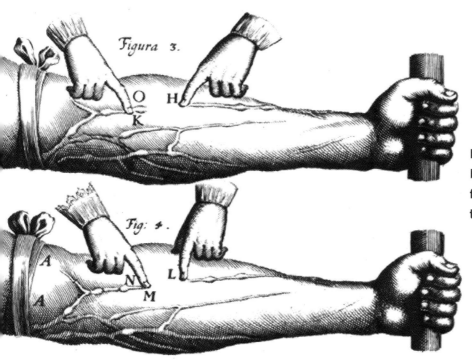

Harvey's drawing of blood vessels showing from underneath the skin.

and the wrist bulge out. He also saw raised parts of the veins, small bumps that were little valves.

Harvey discovered that the entire circulatory system was one big network that recycled the same blood over and over. It was a circular system, and blood traveled around in a giant loop. He also realized the importance of the heart's connection to the lungs in refreshing the blood with oxygen. This fresh blood was sent out through the arteries, and used blood was returned to the heart via the veins.

Just as important, he realized that veins contained tiny valves that allowed the blood to flow in only one direction. This was very different from the belief that blood just washed back and forth in the body like ocean waves. By showing that everything traveled in one direction, Harvey could trace the path of the blood through all the organs, including the kidneys, liver, and spleen, which were important in keeping the blood and the body clean.

Harvey's writings were read by many scientists, and his discoveries changed medicine forever. From that point forward, doctors knew how blood traveled through the body. However, they still didn't know what blood did. After all, Harvey had shown them where the blood went, but not what its purpose was. And it didn't prevent doctors from continuing the popular practice of bloodletting.

In a strange twist of fate, William Harvey died at the age of seventy-nine of a stroke, a condition that is caused by too little blood flowing to the brain.

TRANSFUSING BLOOD

Once the medical community was convinced that blood traveled to all parts of the body in one direction, it decided to start putting things into blood. This was a very risky idea, but doctors thought that if the body responded to certain herbs and fluids that were eaten and ended up in the stomach, then maybe it would be good to put these in the blood. Fortunately for the patients of the day, many of these early tests were tried on animals. Everything from water to wine was inserted into the bloodstream in an effort to see what happened. Scientists quickly found out that these substances do not mix well with blood. The results were usually grim, and the subjects either got very sick or died.

A British physician named Robert Lower hit upon the idea of adding blood to the bloodstream. Perhaps the blood from a healthy individual could be added to the blood of a sick individual, and thus make the sick individual better. This process was called a blood transfusion. He tried it by experimenting with dogs, beginning in 1665. First Lower drained the blood from one dog until it was almost dead. Then, using goose quills as an injection device (syringes with needles hadn't been invented yet), he drained the blood from a second dog into the first one. The first animal recovered with no visible problems. It was the first successful blood transfusion ever.

That experiment led others to think that maybe they could control an imbalance in the humors with different kinds of blood. What if the blood from a nice individual was put into the body of a violent one? Maybe that would make the violent individual more gentle. The blood from a beagle might calm down an angry hound. More important, they wondered, could it be done with humans?

Lower wasn't the one to find out. A Frenchman named

Jean-Baptiste Denis performed blood transfusions between humans and animals.

Jean-Baptiste Denis tried transfusion on a human patient before Lower could (which angered Lower and his British friends to no end). But Denis didn't use human blood on his patient. Like most doctors, he thought that all blood—no matter what the animal—was the same. Dogs and pigs and deer and lions and cows—all had red blood, just like humans. As far as science knew in the 1600s, it was all the same stuff. And it was easy to get blood from a farm animal. There was no reason to take blood from a healthy person and possibly make that person sick. Besides, healthy people needed to keep their own blood "humor" in balance.

In 1667, while Lower and other doctors in England were deciding how to handle the transfusion of blood into humans, a fifteen-year-old boy was brought to Denis. The boy was feverish and faint, and had become very weak. Denis decided that the best thing to do was to transfuse lambs' blood into the boy. Surprisingly, the patient got better. Denis then performed transfusions on three men

shortly thereafter, and it appeared to help them. Other doctors all over Europe started trying transfusions.

However, Denis's fourth patient ultimately died—he had received several transfusions to try to cure his insanity—and the man's wife accused Denis of killing him with the transfusion. She took Denis to court, and the case made headlines all over Europe. People got very nervous about whether transfusions were really a good idea (even though there were signs that the woman had poisoned

Lambs' blood was used in some of the first transfusions.

her husband), and governments throughout Europe soon banned all transfusions.

Like so much that had occurred with blood research prior to the 1800s, Denis had been lucky. Animal blood is actually incompatible with human blood because it has completely different elements in it even though it looks the same. What had probably happened was that Denis's patients' own blood had responded to the invasion of foreign blood by quickly attacking it and trying to destroy it. That's what blood does to keep the body healthy. By triggering this reaction during the transfusion, the patients' bodies may have also overwhelmed the original maladies that the patients were suffering from. But some patients didn't survive, showing that there was something inherently wrong with using animal blood.

After Denis's trial, no one attempted to perform transfusions for nearly two centuries. In the meantime, science finally figured out what blood really was.

CHAPTER 4

Smaller Than Sand

Anton van Leeuwenhoek is one of the most important figures in the entire history of science. He was born in the Netherlands in 1632 and did not go to medical school or study to be a scientist. He made his living making and selling cloth.

One of the tools used in producing cloth during Van Leeuwenhoek's time was a strong magnifying glass. It allowed makers to examine the fine threads and weaving in their cloth to determine how well made it was. Van Leeuwenhoek was so fascinated by these magnifying glasses that he learned how to make them himself. It was not easy; it required that he learn how to handle and shape glass. But Van Leeuwenhoek created a way to make his lenses stronger than those anyone else had ever made. In fact, they were so strong that he could see things that had never been seen before, such as cells and bacteria. What Van Leeuwenhoek had done was create the first working microscopes.

ANTONI VAN LEEUWENHOEK.

Van Leeuwenhoek looked at everything he possibly could, from pieces of stone and coffee beans to saliva and blood. While examining blood, he saw red cells, very distinct objects in the blood that no one knew about. He described their shape and even calculated the size of the cells as "25,000 times smaller than a fine grain of sand." He also was able to see and identify capillaries, the very tiny blood vessels that ran like threads through the human body.

Anton van Leeuwenhoek was the inventor of the microscope.

Several doctors had seen glimpses of these tiny parts of the human body before Van Leeuwenhoek. They had used their own simply constructed microscopes, but no one had the same close-up view—or written up the precise descriptions—that Van Leeuwenhoek had. And he wasn't even a scientist!

Van Leeuwenhoek began sending letters to medical and science groups around Europe. Many of them wouldn't believe or even consider his findings because he was a cloth maker. However, with each discovery—and he made hundreds of them—it appeared that Van Leeuwenhoek had truly done something that scientists had never done before: he had viewed the microscopic world.

Eventually, his microscopes and his studies made Van Leeuwenhoek famous, and he was soon honored all over the globe. He never published books like other scientists—he always put his findings in letters—and remained a cloth maker until he died. He claimed to have pursued his study of the invisible world for the sheer love and wonder of it.

The invention of the microscope and the discovery that blood was made up of tiny cells was exceedingly important

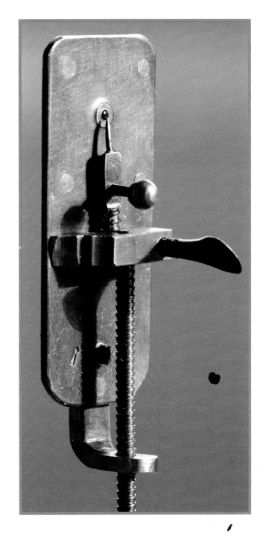

An example of an early microscope by Van Leeuwenhoek.

to scientists. They could now use microscopes to see what blood was made of, and, they hoped, how it behaved and what it did. But they had a long way to go, and doctors continued with many of the practices they had used for years, such as bloodletting.

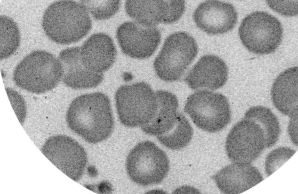

Red blood cells under a microscope.

LETTING GO OF BLOODLETTING

One of the reasons bloodletting had remained popular was that doctors didn't know what else to do—bloodletting had always worked, or so they thought. But doctors and hospitals didn't keep detailed records about how successful bloodletting was. All they knew was that sometimes it worked and sometimes it didn't. They didn't have data on how often bloodletting saved a patient, or even which kinds of patients responded positively to the treatment.

With the discovery that blood was more than just a red liquid that

Most of George Washington's blood was drained from him in the hours before he died.

sloshed around inside the body, doctors and patients started wondering if taking blood was always such a good idea. The question became even more urgent after George Washington was treated with bloodletting— and then died from it.

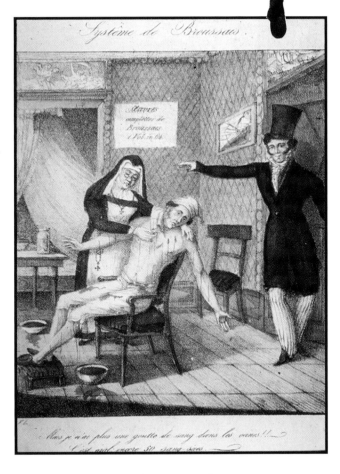

On December 12, 1799, a little over two years after he had finished serving as the first president of the United States, Washington was out riding his horse during a violent winter storm, and didn't bother to take off his wet clothes or warm himself when he returned home. (While nasty weather and dampness do not cause colds, they do weaken the body's immune system, making people vulnerable to attacks by viruses and bacteria.) During the night, he contracted a bad cold, and had a nasty sore throat and fever when he woke up on December 13. His doctors were called, four of them, and decided to start bloodletting, which Washington approved of. Over the course of the next two days, about five pints of Washington's blood were drained from him. That was more than half of all the blood in his body. On the night of December 14, Washington died.

We know now that even a severe cold and sore throat can be treated simply; often bed rest is the best medicine. Bloodletting,

An illustration of a bloodletting procedure.

though, seemed to be the preferred treatment at the time.

However, several of Washington's doctors felt that maybe they had taken too much blood. Washington was sixty-seven years old when he died, and his doctors realized that the massive bloodletting, done over the course of two days, might have been a strain on his body. One of the doctors had actually stated that Washington was too weak to undergo bloodletting, but the other doctors outvoted him. In later years, the doctors privately admitted that bloodletting the former president was a mistake.

Washington's death didn't stop the practice of bloodletting, but it did give doctors a grim reason to start thinking about its supposed benefits more seriously. The procedure continued, perhaps not as frequently as before, but doctors still didn't have anything they thought would work better.

During the mid-1800s, in the years after Washington's bloodletting, scientists proved that the body wasn't controlled by humors or the proper balance of fluids in the body. They discovered that the microorganisms that invaded the body, such as infectious bacteria and viruses, were the main cause of sickness. Microscopes that had improved on Van Leeuwenhoek's design allowed researchers like Louis Pasteur to see how these organisms grew and how they invaded living beings and poisoned food. Pasteur and many others began developing medicines to combat these dangerous organisms.

The ability to fight diseases with specific medicinal drugs significantly changed the way doctors worked. In just a few decades, medicines developed in research labs replaced medical procedures that had been used for centuries. By the end of the 1800s, bloodletting had fallen out of favor with the medical profession, and it died out in most countries. Bloodletting continues to this day in some underdeveloped parts of the world, but it works no better than it did thousands of years ago.

Transfusion

During the 1800s, as the importance of healthy blood became more apparent, doctors realized that blood loss was a very bad thing for humans. Any amount of lost blood—whether by accident or by bloodletting—might be dangerous to a patient's health. One doctor who believed this was a British physician named James Blundell. He had attended to many women who died during childbirth. He felt that in many cases, the amount of blood lost during childbirth might have been a factor in their deaths. There is always a certain amount of blood that a woman loses when giving birth, but Blundell found that the ones who died often had additional bleeding. He wondered if replacing that blood might have saved them.

Despite the international ban on blood transfusions, Blundell began to experiment with ways to put healthy blood back into individuals who had lost a lot of their own blood. Like those before him, he first experimented with dogs, and his research showed some success. In 1818 a man was brought to him who was bleeding internally; the patient was surely going to die if something

A woodcut of a woman in childbirth. In the background, men are reading the stars to predict the baby's future.

wasn't done. Blundell took the opportunity to get blood from several people he worked with, and injected it into the man by using a syringe. The man died anyway.

Despite this failure, Blundell was convinced that blood loss could be corrected by injecting patients with fresh blood. He attempted the process several more times. In most cases, the patients died, but in other cases, the recovery was dramatic. He performed fewer than twelve transfusions altogether, and half the patients—who most certainly would have died otherwise—lived. This was a better percentage of recovery than had been seen during those years when transfusions had been done with animal blood. Plus, Blundell was methodical in his processes, determined to replace lost blood and transfusing not just for the purpose of balancing the humors.

His success rate gave other doctors the courage to start their own investigations into blood transfusion. Many of them used

KARL LANDSTEINER 1868-1943

S 3.50

REPUBLIK ÖSTERREICH

the instruments that Blundell had developed to help with the process, such as devices that safely removed blood from donors before injecting it into a patient.

By the end of the nineteenth century, bloodletting was all but finished and transfusions had become popular again. The success rate was still not as high as most doctors wanted, and they couldn't figure out why. After all, wasn't all human blood the same?

No, it wasn't. It would take one more discovery for the mystery surrounding blood transfusions to be solved.

That discovery came from Karl Landsteiner, a scientist in

Karl Landsteiner discovered that there were several types of blood. His native Austria honored his work by placing his image on a stamp.

Austria. Landsteiner knew a lot about blood. He had performed thousands of autopsies, the procedure that is sometimes used in unusual or mysterious deaths to determine how a person has died. In 1900 Landsteiner saw something strange in his lab, where he was storing blood samples in test tubes. These samples contained blood from different people, all of whom were healthy donors. But the blood in some of the tubes was clumping, forming Jell-O-like particles.

He and others had seen this before, but had figured the clumping occurred only in unhealthy blood. Yet none of these samples had come from sick people. Why was the blood clumping?

Landsteiner began doing experiments in his spare time where he mixed different people's blood samples together. Some clumped up and became gluey, a process called agglutination, and others remained wet and liquid. He studied the blood with a microscope and took copious notes about the samples.

Landsteiner found that some mixed samples got along fine. In others, the red cells from one person exploded when they came into contact with another person's blood. It was a strange reaction: this bursting of blood cells usually happened only when

Blood is stored in test tubes so that it can be viewed and tested.

cells were infected or were trying to fight off disease. Landsteiner determined that in these samples, one blood sample must be fighting off another.

He realized that the blood samples were fighting because they were different. The difference was in a chemical that red blood cells had on their surface to protect them from infection; the presence or absence of this chemical

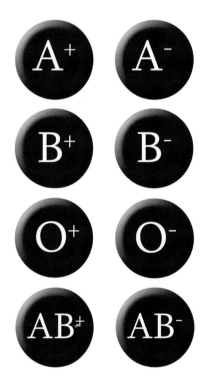

Four types of blood each divided into two groups.

BLOOD TYPES

he four blood types—A, B, AB, and O, known as the ABO blood group—are distinguished by a specific kind of protein found on the outer layer of an individual's red blood cells. It breaks down like this: People with type A blood have a coating of a protein known as an A oligosaccharide attached to their red blood cells. People with type B blood have a coating of B oligosaccharide attached to their red blood cells (RBCs). People who are type AB have both A and B oligosaccharides on their RBCs. People with type O have neither A nor B oligosaccharides in their blood. These types are determined by a person's genetic makeup and cannot be changed.

An interesting thing occurs within these groups, though. While it is best to match blood types—such as with type A getting a transfusion from someone with type A—some of these types are interchangeable. For example, people with type AB blood can use blood from every other group, but no one

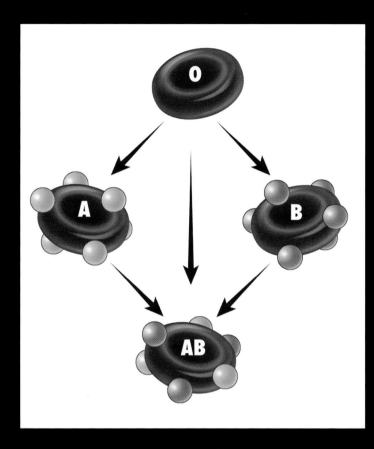

Blood donors recipients

The blood of rhesus monkeys led
to the discovery of "positive" and
"negative" blood types in humans.

else can use type AB. People with O blood must get blood from another O person, but O blood can be used with all other types. For this reason, type AB is called universal recipient blood and type O is called universal donor blood.

Below the ABO category is a subgroup based on what is called the Rh factor. Your Rh factor is determined by whether or not your blood has a particular molecule that fights off certain kinds of cells, such as those produced by bacteria. If you have this molecule, then your blood is called positive. If you don't have it, the blood is typed as negative. So a person who has type O blood without the Rh factor is type O negative. The term "Rh factor" comes from the initial discovery of this molecule in the blood of rhesus monkeys.

created four kinds of blood. Landsteiner and his assistants called these blood types A, B, AB, and O. It turned out that everyone in the world had blood that fell into one of these four primary groups.

With the knowledge that people had different types of blood, the approach to transfusions took a huge turn. Doctors now understood that they had to put the correct blood type into their patients. It wasn't the method of transfusion that had been causing problems; it was the fact that different blood types attacked each other when they came into contact. When that happened, patients died.

Using a simple test that involved mixing the patient's blood with known samples to see whether it clumped or not, doctors could quickly determine the correct blood type. Suddenly transfusions were saving many lives. This was especially true in the

A wounded U.S. soldier is given a blood transfusion during World War I.

A pint of Your Blood

MAY SAVE A SOLDIERS LIFE

DONATE YOUR BLOOD
and American boys
will get the blood
plasma they need!

CALL
Murray Hill 5-6400

for an appointment

RED CROSS BLOOD DONOR CENTER
2 E. 37th STREET   NEW YORK CITY

last few years of World War I, when blood was used throughout
Europe to help injured soldiers who had lost a lot of it on the
battlefield. By that time, people had started donating their own
blood to help save the lives of the troops.

It had been nearly three hundred years from the days of

A Red Cross poster asking for blood donations to help soldiers in wartime.

animal blood transfusions, which routinely killed patients, to a world in which the blood from one person could immediately save the life of another. Science and medicine had finally found out how essential blood was to keeping people healthy, and how to use it to help them recover from serious injuries and illnesses. Blood transfusions became one of the most important medical procedures ever invented.

There was no longer any doubt that blood was the most important part of the body. Technology had allowed scientists and doctors to uncover the mysteries hidden in blood. Now you're going to discover exactly what your blood does as it makes its way through every part of you.

CHAPTER 5

Making Blood

he best way to describe what blood is and does is to follow it through the body. As you read the next few chapters, take a moment to stop every once in a while and think about the fact that everything we'll be talking about is happening in your body right this instant. Stop to feel your heartbeat or to consider the blood flowing into your brain and through your liver. Look at the pulse of blood thumping through your wrist—and then touch it to feel the flow. Look at the bluish veins in your feet below your ankles and check out the red vessels in your eyes.

It's often difficult to think about the incredible things that blood does because you never see any of them, even though they are going on right under your skin. Blood touches everything in your body, from your eyes to your intestines. What is most significant about your blood is how it interacts with everything it comes into contact with. This includes the organs it passes through, the nutrients it carries, and even the diseases that it can sometimes spread. Everything begins, and ends, with blood.

Where does blood itself begin? Inside your bones.

The hard outer part of bones protects a soft, spongy material called the marrow. You can see marrow if you break open a chicken bone; it's darker than the outside of the bone and has a different texture. Your marrow is dark red and is filled with stem cells, which are your body's master control cells. They can produce any other kind of cell, depending on what your body needs. In the marrow, stem cells' job is to create red and white blood cells as well as platelets.

Your bone marrow creates nearly three million red blood cells every second. The average red blood cell lives about four months before it wears out and needs to be replaced. If red blood cells weren't replenished quickly, you would suffer from a condition called anemia, which happens when there are too few red blood cells in your bloodstream.

Red blood cells (also known as RBCs, erythrocytes, and corpuscles) are unusual

Your skeletal system is the source of new blood.

because after they are created, they lose their nucleus. Most cells have a nucleus, which acts like each cell's brain, but RBCs need that space so that hemoglobin can carry as much oxygen as possible. And moving oxygen throughout your body is the primary function of each red blood cell.

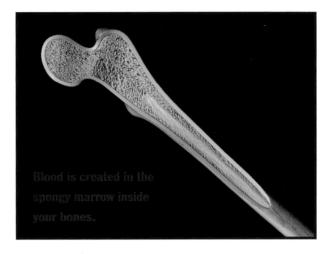

Blood is created in the spongy marrow inside your bones.

Once red blood cells are formed, they join with white blood cells (called leukocytes) and platelets—also made in the marrow—and start working their way out of the bone and into the bloodstream. This is done via minuscule blood vessels called capillaries, which reach out like small branches from your main blood vessels, the veins and arteries.

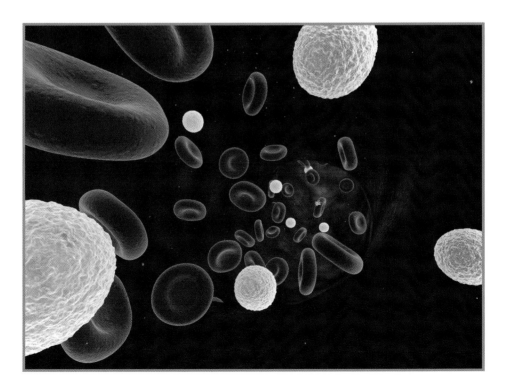

All the components of your blood merge in the bloodstream.

Capillaries go into all the tight places that larger vessels cannot, especially in your skin. Some are as thick as a human hair, and others are like microscopic threads—so small that they allow only one cell at a time to pass through. When you see blood from a scrape or a pinprick on your skin, you know that tiny capillaries have been ripped open. Because they are so small, they don't typically gush a lot of blood.

When new blood cells enter the bloodstream, they must get to the heart and lungs so they can begin their work. This means traveling through the circulatory system.

The circulatory system is one big network, but it has two distinct parts. The first part is called the pulmonary loop, which is controlled by the right side of your heart. In this loop, your heart pumps blood to your lungs and back again so your blood can dump carbon dioxide and then pick up oxygen. (The process of the heart and lungs working together is called the cardiopulmonary system.)

The second part of the circulatory system is called the systemic loop, which is controlled by the left side of the heart. This is the path that the blood uses to go from your heart out to your body and back again, delivering oxygen to organs and muscles and picking up carbon dioxide.

In the pulmonary loop, blood enters the right side of the heart through a large vein called the vena cava. It goes into the

Capillaries are so thin that they permeate your entire body. They would extend tens of thousands of miles if laid out end to end.

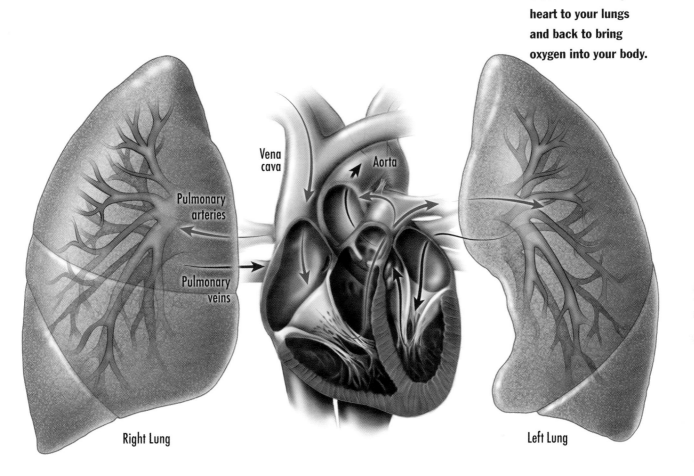

Blood flows from your heart to your lungs and back to bring oxygen into your body.

Vena cava

Aorta

Pulmonary arteries

Pulmonary veins

Right Lung

Left Lung

top part of the heart and rushes into an open chamber called the right atrium. When the heart contracts (the first thump that you hear when your heart beats), the blood is forced down through an opening into another chamber called the right ventricle. Once it gets there, a fleshy valve closes to keep the blood from flowing backwards. Remember, in your body, blood always flows in one direction and never flows backwards.

The blood is then forced from the right ventricle out of the heart (the second part of the thump-thump) through a blood vessel

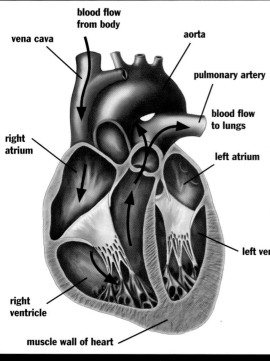

blood flow from body

vena cava

aorta

pulmonary artery

blood flow to lungs

right atrium

left atrium

left ventricle

right ventricle

muscle wall of heart

called the pulmonary artery. This leads the blood into capillaries in your lungs. Here is where the blood starts its real work.

The blood flushes into all the capillaries in the lungs, which are housed in little broccoli-shaped protrusions known as alveoli.

Blood returns to your heart through the vena cava.

BLOOD PRESSURE AND PULSE

our blood pressure is a measure of how hard your blood is pressing against your blood vessels. This is important because it tells doctors and nurses if your heart is beating at the appropriate strength and if there are potential problems with your arteries' being clogged.

Blood pressure is recorded using two numbers. The first is systolic pressure, which is the pressure that occurs when your heart beats, forcing blood through your body. The second is the diastolic pressure, the pressure that happens when the heart is between beats and is not forcing blood into your arteries. The numbers are based on the force, or pressure, that blood exerts on the walls of the blood vessels as it flows through them. The numbers are reported in millimeters. For adults, an average number is 120 systolic and 80 diastolic, usually read as "120 over 80."

Your pulse is something different altogether. It is an indicator of how many times per minute your heart is beating. You can check your own pulse by placing a finger or two gently on "pulse points," where your arteries are close to the surface of your skin. These include the front of your wrist just under your thumb and the crook of your elbow. After exercise, you'll notice that your pulse rate goes way up due to your heart's working harder. If you're sleepy, your pulse will slow down.

There are anywhere from 300 to 700 million alveoli in the lungs; your lungs have that many alveoli because they need to expose as many capillaries to air as possible.

When you take a breath, fresh air comes into your lungs. As your lungs fill up, air passes over the alveoli and the capillaries. Hemoglobin attracts oxygen molecules to itself from out of the air and binds itself to them. Once the hemoglobin is filled with oxygen, it turns the RBCs bright red.

The next beat of the heart pushes this oxygen-fresh blood out of your lungs so that another supply of blood can come in. The fresh blood flows back into your heart, only it goes into the left side this time. It flows into the left atrium through your pulmonary vein. When the left atrium is filled, the blood flows down into the left ventricle. Again, valves keep the blood from flowing backwards.

As your heart beats, the fresh blood is pumped out of the left ventricle through the aorta. This is the body's largest blood vessel, almost an inch wide. The force of blood going through the aorta is incredible. It could easily squirt your blood across a room if it weren't enclosed inside your body. This force is necessary to push the blood through the thousands of miles of vessels that are woven throughout your body.

After leaving your aorta, the blood enters the circulatory system. Think of the circulatory system as a river with tributaries and streams branching off it. Instead of all the liquid just going down one big river, it flows into various branches all at the same time. Those branches of the river split off into other,

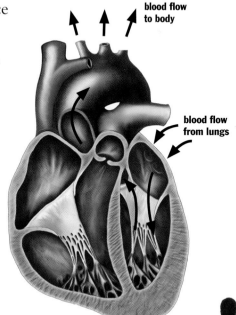

blood flow to body

blood flow from lungs

After being filled with oxygen, blood is pushed back into your body through your aorta.

smaller branches, and finally into little streams and brooks where the flow is barely a trickle. The same thing happens with blood. It pushes into all available arteries, and then it works its way, via small arteries called arterioles, into your brain and other organs. The route gets even smaller as the arterioles branch into the capillaries.

Once blood gets moving, it has a long trip ahead of it . . . through miles and miles of your body.

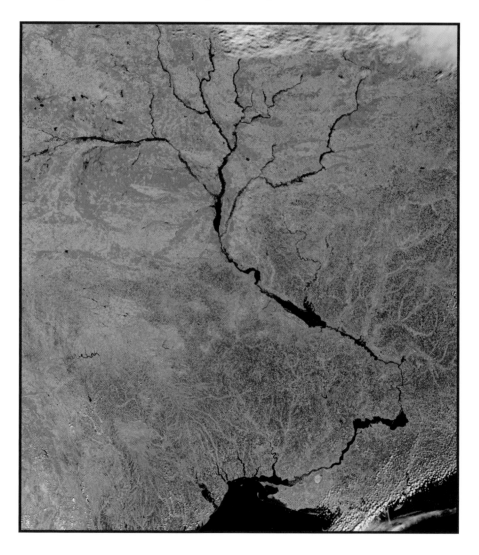

This satellite photo shows a river with tributaries that allow the water to branch out into the smallest areas. In the same way, the circulatory system branches out through your body with veins, arteries, and capillaries.

CHAPTER 6

Where the Blood Flows

Blood carries oxygen to every part of the body, especially the brain, which gets 20 percent of all the blood coming out of the heart. Other organs also get a substantial amount, as do the muscles. While blood is moving, oxygen separates from hemoglobin and is absorbed by cells in the organs. These cells use oxygen to keep themselves alive and perform their own chemical processes.

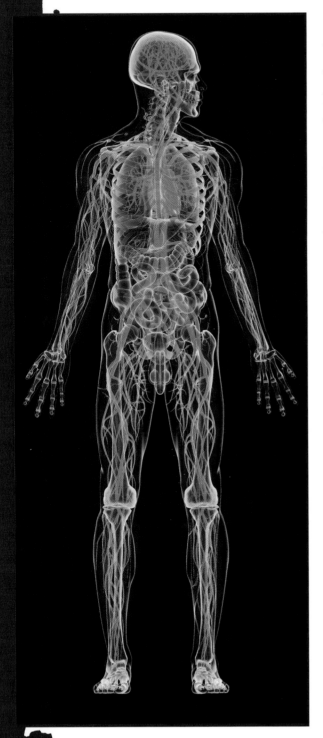

RBCs eventually squeeze into the smallest capillaries, wide enough to allow only single cells to pass through. Here, the last of the oxygen is given up. At this point in the journey, the capillaries connect to similarly small vessels called venules, or little veins. This is where the deoxygenated blood begins to make its return trip to the heart.

Because the oxygen is gone, blood loses its bright red color. It is now a weird maroon-purple color. After leaving oxygen behind, the RBCs start attracting carbon dioxide molecules. These are the waste molecules that organs and tissue cells get rid of while they're doing their work (such as growing, helping your muscles move, and making your nervous system respond to commands from your brain). As it binds with carbon dioxide, blood moves from the capillaries to the venules and on to the veins.

Just as arteries take blood away from the heart, veins deliver blood back to the heart. But

The circulatory system is the highway by which your blood reaches every part of your body.

unlike the thick stream of blood that rushes through the aorta at the start of its journey, the blood begins its return trip as single cells working their way through microscopic venules. And instead of flowing from the main circulatory river out into branches, it travels back from the little branches to ever bigger branches until it joins the main flow of blood through the veins. These veins then converge and send the blood on to the vena cava, where it enters the right side of the heart.

This carbon dioxide–filled blood is forced from the heart's right ventricle into the lungs. There it goes into the alveoli. Now think back: we started this story with you taking a breath, bringing air into your lungs, and filling up the alveoli with oxygen. The end of the journey, or what happens before you take that new breath of fresh oxygen, is that you exhale, forcing air out of your lungs. When you breathe out, the lungs remove carbon dioxide from the blood before refreshing it with oxygen. That's why you breathe out carbon dioxide and breathe in oxygen. It's as if your blood is a riverboat unloading the waste an instant before being loaded up with fresh and valuable cargo.

This whole process takes about thirty seconds. That seems like a very short period of time for a gallon of blood to make an entire circuit through the body. Keep in mind that you have a lot of blood, and not all of it goes straight to the same place each time it leaves the heart. It is all flowing continuously; there are no gaps or spaces between the blood as it moves. It's happening nonstop, like a hose that's been left on.

Even though blood's main function is to carry oxygen, that's not the only thing it does. What blood does when it reaches certain organs, and what certain organs do to the blood, is an entirely different side of our story.

THE OTHER SIDE

Everything you put in your body ends up in your blood. Food, medicine, air, water—all are plucked from your stomach, lungs, and small intestines by blood. Because each of your organs has its own function, the way it interacts with your blood is very different.

THE BRAIN

The brain needs more blood than any other part of your body because every part of your body depends on the brain working properly. Without blood and oxygen, the brain quickly grows weak, which can result in brain damage or death. And without your brain telling everything how to work, your body will shut down, like a car without any gas or electricity.

Almost 20 percent of all the fresh blood coming out of your heart goes straight to your brain. The carotid arteries, which run up both sides of your neck, are two of the most important blood vessels in your body because they provide the biggest rush of blood straight to your brain.

To make sure that blood always gets to your brain, there is a ring of arterial connections that provide additional pathways into the brain. The ring is called the Circle of Willis. It is named after Thomas Willis, a physician who

More blood goes to your brain than to any other place in your body.

wrote the first textbook on the brain, in 1664. It's very easy to recognize the ring because it looks like a human stick figure with a large head. The many pathways in the Circle of Willis ensure that blood gets into the brain even if one artery is damaged or blocked.

Most of the blood work in the brain occurs in a three-layered brain wrapping called the meninges. The layers of the meninges are the pia, arachnoid, and dura.

The dura is basically like bubble wrap for the brain. It cushions the brain and prevents it from moving around inside your skull. Underneath that is the arachnoid layer, which contains crisscrossing blood vessels that look very much like a spider web. In fact, it is called the arachnoid layer because of the scientific name for spiders, which is "arachnid." The blood vessels in the arachnoid weave through your cerebrospinal fluid, a clear liquid that floats around your brain. Cerebrospinal fluid has many purposes, one of the most important being that it flows through small spaces in the brain and keeps it clean by removing any garbage that accumulates, such as dead cells. This waste soaks back into the bloodstream via the arachnoid

The Circle of Willis ensures that blood gets to the brain by a number of different routes.

and is washed out of your head.

The third meninges layer is called the pia mater. It is the layer closest to the brain and fits snugly around the whole brain like a piece of plastic shrink-wrap. The pia contains the primary blood vessels that supply fuel—glucose and oxygen—to the brain. At the same time, the pia also picks up cell waste and brings it back into the bloodstream for disposal.

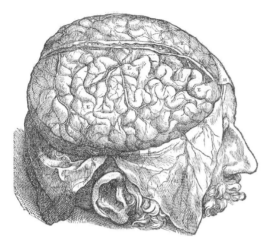

This illustration shows that the meninges cover the brain like wrapping paper so that not even blood can get through.

The interesting thing is that blood goes into the pia, but never actually enters the main parts of the brain. These parts, the cerebrum, cerebellum, and medulla, are where thinking, dreaming, and body control take place. Blood doesn't get to them because of what is known as the blood-brain barrier. This barrier is made up of blood vessels that are so tiny, only molecules of oxygen and glucose can squeeze through. Not even RBCs or germs can pass the barrier. It's like a water filter: it lets only the pure stuff enter the brain.

THE SMALL INTESTINE

The nutrients that are so essential to your brain and the rest of your body come by way of the food you put into your mouth every day. Once food has been partially digested in the stomach, it makes its way to the small intestine, which is a coiled tube more than twenty feet long. In the small intestine, food is broken down even further, with help from digestive juices supplied by your pancreas and liver. Much of this is done with a strong acidlike chemical called bile. What remains after this breakdown is a watery, liquid full of various nutrients such as sugars and salts, along with fats, vitamins, minerals, and other substances. This liquid is the raw fuel that your body needs.

The inside of the small intestine is lined with hairlike projections called villi. Like the alveoli in the lungs, they are full of capillaries. The villi soak up the nutrient liquid from the small intestine, and this liquid enters the capillaries. From there the nutrients go to the liver to be cleaned, and then flow to other organs in the body to be used with oxygen as fuel by the cells.

Anything that the blood doesn't need from the small intestine heads out to the large intestine and is passed out of your body.

THE LIVER

The liver is the largest organ in your body and looks like a slightly squashed football. It is tucked in above your stomach on the right side. It's one of the most complex organs, involved in as many as five hundred body processes. The liver is also the only organ that can repair itself—and grow back its parts—after being damaged.

The liver is essential to blood for a number of reasons, especially because it makes sure that blood is carrying the right substances to the rest of the body. The chemicals in the liver go after

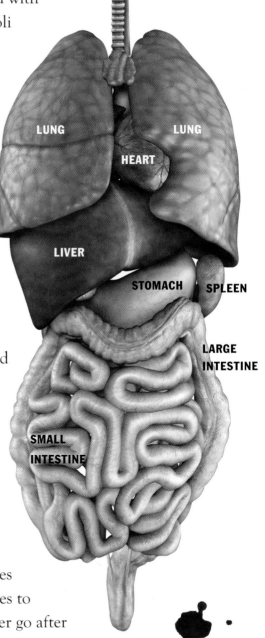

LUNG

LUNG

HEART

LIVER

STOMACH   SPLEEN

LARGE
INTESTINE

SMALL
INTESTINE

Everything you put into your mouth ends up in your blood . . . and these are the organs that play a vital role in helping blood do its job.

The liver is your blood system's biggest filter.

LIVER

SPLEEN

STOMACH

anything that doesn't belong in your blood and breaks it down.

When blood leaves the villi and capillaries in the small intestine, it heads to the liver. Blood enters the liver through two pathways. The first is the hepatic portal vein ("hepatic" comes from the Greek word for liver, *"hepar"*). At the same time, the hepatic artery is also bringing oxygen-rich blood into the liver. This means that blood from the heart and blood on its way back to the heart are passing through the liver at the same time. The liver is the one place where arterial and venous blood mix together so they can be cleaned simultaneously.

Chemicals in the liver break down the substances that shouldn't be in the blood and filter them out. These include caffeine, alcohol, many drugs, bacteria, and even random particles that may have found their way into your blood. They could be anything from food molecules to dirt that might have slipped past your small intestine or entered your body through a wound. The liver also adds a protein called fibrinogen to the blood. Fibrinogen is the basis for fibrin, a threadlike substance that floats in the bloodstream and forms a kind of net when external bleeding occurs. Fibrin is one of the things that create blood clots and keep you from bleeding to death when you are injured.

Your liver works so hard that it filters nearly a third of all your blood every minute. The clean blood from the liver flows back to the heart via the hepatic vein. After the clean blood is gone, the dead and diseased blood cells remain. The liver breaks them down into a substance called bilirubin, which is dark brown due to the color of the used-up RBCs. All of this waste then flows to the large intestine to be sent on its way to the local bathroom. By the way, all those dead RBCs that make up bilirubin are the reason why feces are brown.

If it wasn't for your liver, you could never have been born. When a baby is still inside the mother, the baby's liver helps create new blood cells before the bone marrow has fully developed. So the first blood your body created for itself came from your liver.

THE SPLEEN

The spleen is one of those organs you don't hear much about. Many people don't even know what it does—even scientists didn't know a lot about it until recently.

The spleen is a squishy purplish organ located just to the left of your stomach. Like the kidneys and liver, it spends much of its time acting as a blood filter. It is full of blood, which it stores in open spaces and receives from the heart through the splenic artery.

Rather than filtering out toxins or other substances, the spleen's real work involves the components of the blood itself. It detects worn-out or damaged red and white blood cells, as well as platelets. Once blood cells are unable to function

Your spleen is small, but it acts as a blood reservoir in times of emergency.

properly, the spleen destroys them, making them completely useless. The spleen then recycles any usable parts, such as iron, in the blood. The rest is passed on to the liver through the portal vein so it can be removed from the body as waste.

Because it can hold a lot of blood all at once, the spleen also serves as a miniature blood reservoir. In times when the body is sick or injured and is losing blood, the spleen can squeeze some of its stored-up reserves back into the body so that the proper amount is still flowing through the arteries and veins. When the body's blood level is back to normal again, the spleen restocks its reservoir.

The spleen is also one of the first lines of defense for the blood. It produces a very specific type of white blood cell called lymphocytes, which are disease fighters. If the spleen discovers viruses or parasites in the blood, it ramps up the production of these white blood cells. These cells then attack the invaders in the bloodstream in an attempt to kill them off before they can do harm to the rest of the body. Other white cells in the spleen can actually devour bacteria and fungi.

The spleen is one of the few organs you can live without—although it's better to have one—because other organs like the liver are able take over some of its duties.

THE KIDNEYS

The kidneys are two bean-shaped organs located on the left and right side of your body just above your stomach. Their job is to clean out waste material picked up from cells and organs by the blood as it flows through your body.

In addition to carbon dioxide, the bloodstream—primarily the plasma—gets filled up with dead cells, cell byproducts, and other junk as it makes its way all over the body. Blood has to be cleaned out somewhere along the line, or it would be full of waste. The kidneys serve as the equivalent of the local garbage dump.

The kidneys receive almost 20 percent of the blood pushed out from the heart, nearly as much as the brain. The blood enters the kidneys via the renal artery. Since so much blood is entering the kidneys, it is forced through capillaries and hundreds of thousands of tubelike structures called nephrons. As the blood moves through the nephrons, waste products are squeezed out of the plasma, just like a coffee filter that catches the grinds in a coffee maker or a juicer that traps the pulp from oranges. Any nutrients that remain are absorbed back into the bloodstream, since they can still be used.

The kidneys take out excess molecules that you might have in your blood from eating too much of any particular kind of food.

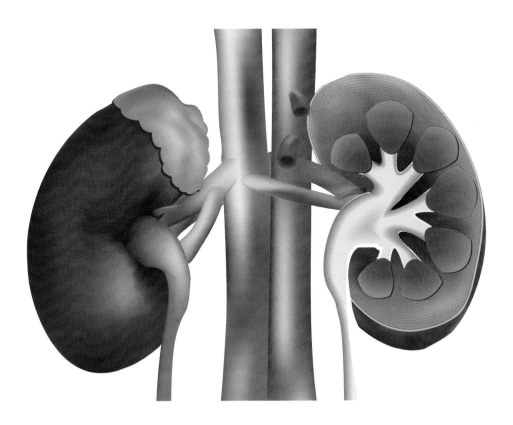

Kidneys receive nearly twice as much blood from the heart as the brain does, which is almost 20 percent of your blood.

This is especially true of foods with a lot of sugar and salt. The remains of used-up medicines also end up in your kidneys.

The kidneys are the only place where blood makes a jump from arteries directly to veins without going through the intricate mesh of capillaries and venules. The clean blood from the kidneys then flows back into the bloodstream to continue its way to the heart. The leftover waste is mixed with water and other chemicals and discharged from your body as urine.

This journey around the circulatory system has shown you how blood nourishes and fuels your body. There is a dark side of blood, however, and it can lead to serious problems in your body.

CHAPTER 7

The Blood's Battleground

Your blood is more responsible for keeping you alive than anything else in your body. You've just seen how blood makes its way from place to place, working every second of every day of your life to make sure your body functions as it is supposed to.

That's the nice, normal part of blood. And when things are going well for our bodies, we can go months or years without thinking about what blood does for us.

It's only when we get sick or seriously hurt that blood comes rushing back into our thoughts—or rushing out of our bodies.

From our blood's perspective, the body is not only something to be serviced, it is also something to be protected. And there are occasions when your blood has to act like an army, going out to attack invaders, fight off infections, destroy bacteria, defend against disease, detect and kill intruders, and stand guard until your body is healed. It sounds violent, and at the microscopic level, it truly is.

Blood is just as vital to us in times of sickness as it is in health. We can see that when we get something as minor as a simple paper cut or accidentally get poked with a sharp object. That's when blood comes, literally, to the surface.

When something sharp cuts your skin, or if you fall on a rough surface that scrapes your skin, it tears through several layers of flesh called the epidermis. Like the rest of your body, there are millions of capillaries of all sizes woven through these layers (except for the very top layers of skin, which is why if you scratch your skin lightly you won't bleed). This tear, cut, or scrape also rips into the capillaries, opening them up as if you were slicing into a water pipe or a straw. Once that happens, blood leaks out. Some capillaries are bigger than others, so in some places the blood flow is heavier and faster.

Once the blood hits the air, it turns a very bright bright red, even if it's already given up much of its oxygen inside the body. That's because it's absorbing the oxygen outside your body.

When a blood vessel is damaged and RBCs are exposed to air, platelets get very busy very quickly. The torn vessel releases a substance called collagen that the platelets react to. Since collagen is inside the walls of the vessel, it is normally kept away from platelets. But once collagen comes into contact with the bloodstream, the platelets start bunching up together, blocking the flow of red and white cells. At the same time, the torn blood vessels squeeze tight, reducing blood flow.

As platelets get exposed to the air, they break apart and spread out, creating a sticky mass. Little bits of fibrinogen that the liver produces join the mass. They mix with the platelets and form little threads of fibrin. The fibrin weaves around the platelets and creates a net that holds the mass together. Together, they form a blockade that prevents the red and white blood cells from passing through. This is called coagulation.

Once the blood has been sealed off, this blockade forms a clot. The blood changes from a flowing liquid to a sticky and barely moving mass. As this mass hardens, it forms a scab. You're familiar with scabs; they're the hard little shells that cover a cut or scrape. A scab gets harder as air dries it out, and it becomes

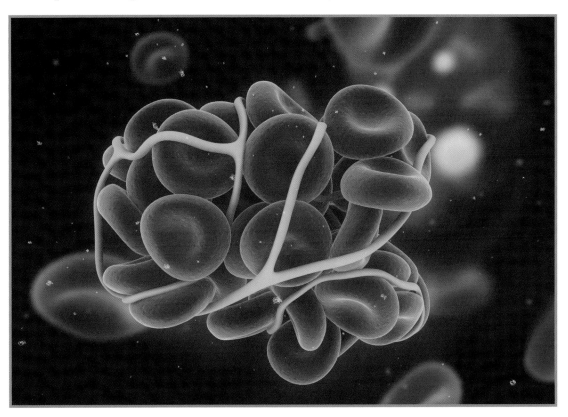

Creating a clot: fibrin forms a net that prevents red blood cells from leaking out of the body.

a protective coating for the damaged vessel while the vessel is repaired with new cells.

When the situation is under control, the collagen stops seeping into the blood, and blood flow continues as normal. After about two weeks, there is no visible sign that anything even happened to your skin. The body is so good at repairing itself that the damage completely disappears. (In extreme cases, a wound may remove a large and deep section of skin. When this happens, the repair process leaves a scar in the area that it patches up, much like the bunching up that occurs when thread is used to repair a tear in cloth.)

This is what occurs when you have minor injuries. These almost always involve capillaries. It is rare that you will ever have the kind of injury that would sever a major artery or vein. Most of the vessels are buried deeper in the body, closer to organs and bones. If these are damaged, though, the blood flow is usually too fast for the coagulants to work, and has to be slowed down by other means. Usually this involves pressure being placed on the bleeding area to squish the vessel shut. People giving first aid will accomplish this by using the palms of their hands to press down on the wound. If the injury is extreme, a doctor will wrap a tight bandage, called a tourniquet, around the place where the injury has occurred—say an arm or a leg—so that the artery is pressed shut to stop the blood. Eventually the wound itself has to be closed, and a doctor will seal it with stitches.

You probably cause minor damage to your body regularly without even thinking about it. Scratching mosquito bites, accidentally biting your lip, bumping your nose, stepping on something sharp—all these are ways that blood makes its way to the outside of your body. Because blood works so well, you usually forget about these incidents shortly after it stops flowing.

Pressure is one way to prevent blood loss because it squeezes the blood vessels closed.

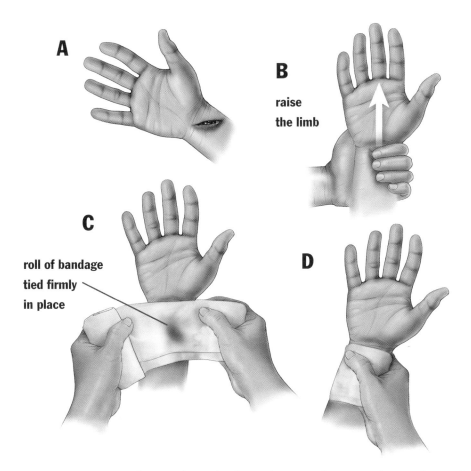

A

B

raise the limb

C

roll of bandage tied firmly in place

D

Some people aren't so lucky. They are born without the right kind of elements in their blood to create clots. This condition is called hemophilia. When hemophiliacs get even a tiny cut, their blood can't stop flowing. Their bodies aren't able to produce the fibrin that is so important to creating the clots that block blood flow. Without clots, the blood just keeps going and going. Fortunately, hemophiliacs can inject the necessary blood parts into their bloodstream using a medicine that is made of blood obtained from other people. This mixes with their own blood to provide coagulants in case they do start bleeding. But since all blood components eventually break down in the body, hemophiliacs have to take a regular supply of this medicine to avoid any problems should they injure themselves.

Blood clotting and the resultant scabbing is the only example of blood healing we can see with our own eyes. The rest of it happens *inside* our bodies. Even then, this happens at the microscopic level, and we couldn't observe it even if we wanted to. Interestingly, while the repairs we can see happen with RBCs, the repairs that occur inside us are all about the white blood cells.

ON THE ATTACK

If RBCs and plasma are the couriers that deliver important packages such as oxygen and nutrients to your organs and tissues, white blood cells are the soldiers that protect those deliveries. Not only do they act as bodyguards for the RBCs, but they serve as scouts that go out to destroy invaders that might want to get into your body and hurt it.

White blood cells come in five main types, and they are all part of your immune system. The immune system is the name for all the organs, tissues, and chemicals in your body that protect you from sickness. The things that cause sickness come in many different forms. A virus that enters your body can cause pneumonia. Bacteria can bring diseases like anthrax and the plague into your system. A malfunction in your normal body processes can cause cancer. White blood cells have to be prepared for all this and much more.

Each type of white blood cell focuses on a specific

FIVE TYPES OF
WHITE BLOOD CELLS

There are five primary types of white blood cells (WBCs), each with a specific job to do when your body is attacked by disease or becomes infected by a cut. Depending on what your body needs, the amount of any one type of WBC varies. For instance, if you have a bacterial infection, your body will produce more neutrophils than lymphocytes.

- **NEUTROPHILS** are the most plentiful WBCs, usually accounting for at least half of the WBCs in your body at any given time. They fight off infection from fungi and bacteria and are the primary element of pus.

- **EOSINOPHILS** make up only about 5 percent of all WBCs. They defend against parasites and cause inflammation during allergic reactions.

- **BASOPHILS** react to allergy-causing invaders by creating histamines that cause inflammation around the source of the invasion, such as the nose and mouth. They make up less than 1 percent of all WBCs.

- **LYMPHOCYTES** are the second-largest group of WBCs, sometimes making up 50 percent of your white blood cell count. They are important in killing viruses and cancerous cells.

- **MONOCYTES** account for a little over 1 percent of your WBCs. Their job is to "eat up" solid particles and cell waste and then remove it from the bloodstream.

function, although some of the WBCs' duties overlap. The basic function of white blood cells is to identify a problem or an invading microorganism (like a virus), signal to other white cells for help, and then band together in a large group to attack the invader.

Imagine that a simple yet unwanted virus like a rhinovirus has

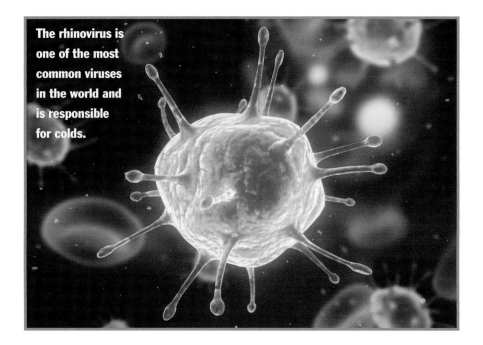

The rhinovirus is one of the most common viruses in the world and is responsible for colds.

entered your body. You don't have to imagine too hard because it's already happened to you: the rhinovirus causes the common cold. It floats in water droplets in the air when other people who have a cold sneeze, or it lives on their hands or on things they've touched, like doorknobs. You might breathe it in, or you might get it from shaking hands and then rubbing your nose or eyes. Once the rhinovirus gets in your body, it digs into your cells and starts reproducing. This usually happens in the lining of breathing passages way up in your nose and sinuses.

The cells damaged by the virus release chemicals that cause the surrounding blood vessels to swell. This leads to a condition known as inflammation. Inflammation happens because the blood vessels need to handle a larger flow of white blood cells to the infected area. You can see inflammation on your skin when it turns red from an infection, or in the bright redness of your throat when you're sick. Even sunburn is an inflammation of the skin. Inflammation also occurs internally. Tennis elbow, for example, is caused by an inflammation of the tendons around your elbow from the strain of hitting a ball the same way too many times.

After the rhinovirus has invaded your cells, it begins multiplying very quickly in the nice, warm, and wet portions of your nose and throat. Inflammation, caused by your blood vessels opening up, brings white blood cells right to where the rhinovirus is. But this makes you feel congested because the blood vessels are swelling, and that irritates the area around your nose and throat. You may also get a fever. Scientists aren't sure why we get fevers, but they believe that an increase in body temperature helps to kill off invading viruses and also speeds up the reaction of the immune system.

All of these are symptoms of a cold, but here's an interesting thing to note: The virus isn't what makes you feel bad. It's a sad truth that what makes you so miserable when you have a cold is the violent way in which your body has to act against viruses to make sure they don't get to your vital organs and cause more damage. The virus just sets off the whole process.

As soon as white blood cells reach the rhinovirus, they take immediate action. Depending on the kind of white blood cells activated, they go after the virus in a number of ways. Some white blood cells, like neutrophils, eat your infected cells and thus devour the virus within them. Lymphocytes can attack the virus and attempt to chemically break it down, almost like the way acid breaks down metal. White blood cells also release a protein called an antibody. This binds to the virus and keeps it from reproducing, thus isolating it and killing it.

**When you get a cold, blood rushes to the affected areas,
causing inflammation from your nose to your throat.**

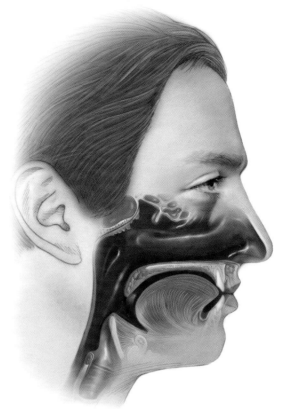

The rhinovirus, for its part, keeps trying to reproduce fast enough to stay ahead of the attacking white cells. It, too, wants to survive at any cost.

After a few days of this battle, the rhinovirus is defeated. All of your body's defense mechanisms return to normal, and you start to feel better. This is always the case, because you always recover after a cold.

The rhinovirus is a good example of an invader for several reasons: It is a relatively common virus and ultimately very weak. It rarely causes serious illness because it is easily overwhelmed by your white blood cells and immune system (although it doesn't feel "easy" while you're sick). In addition, the common cold and the rhinovirus cannot be "cured" or destroyed by medicine. Science has still not figured out a way to create a drug that can kill the virus once it's in your body. That's why you can't get a shot or take a pill to make a cold go away. The medicines people do take, like aspirin or cough syrup, help ease the symptoms, but they don't take care of the cause.

This is important because there are many times when your blood needs help in attacking a disease. Some viruses, bacteria, and even poisons—from poisonous plants or animals like venomous snakes—are so strong that the blood can't fight them off by itself. In the days before modern medicine, people died regularly from these infections. The flu, the plague, smallpox, polio, and pneumonia were fatal or permanently crippling diseases for most of human history. They were unstoppable, until the development in the early 1900s of antibiotics—drugs such as penicillin that kill bacteria—gave humans a better chance of surviving disease.

These drugs either enter the bloodstream through your mouth, in the form of a liquid or pill, or are injected right into your blood. They do much of the same work that white blood cells do. The difference is that these medicines are designed to kill specific viruses, parasites, and fungi by traveling through the blood and killing all the invaders in their path.

The odd thing in most deadly diseases is that they use the bloodstream to do their dirty work. Once they get into the body, they fight off all the body's defenses and destroy white blood cells until they can travel freely in the blood and invade organs such as the lungs and the brain. If white blood cells can't kill them off, these diseases travel in the plasma directly to the places where they can do the most damage.

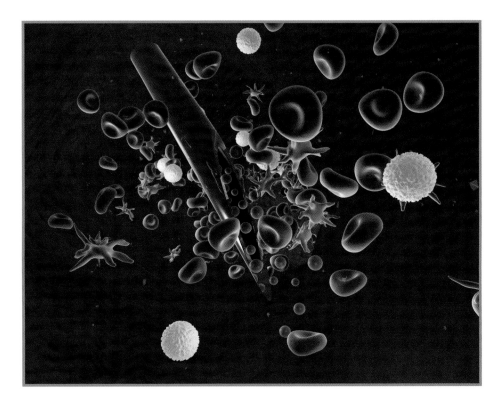

A good example is meningitis. This is an infection of the meninges, the protective layer around the brain. It is usually caused by a bacterium called *Neisseria meningitidis*. This dangerous form of bacteria is spread from person to person by very close contact such as sneezing, coughing, and kissing. Meningitis is extremely rare, but also extremely deadly because it can eat away your blood vessels and cause damage to your brain.

Because it is so dangerous, your body responds extremely violently to it. Vomiting, fever, and uncontrollable body movements (called seizures) are all symptoms of meningitis. The bacterium is incredibly strong, and it often defeats all of the white blood cells that try to attack it. Eventually, hordes of bacteria make their way to the brain, where they eat through the blood-brain barrier. This allows the bacteria to get into the brain, and also causes blood

Some medicines are injected directly into your bloodstream, where they merge with your blood to fight diseases and infections. The medicine is shown here as blue droplets coming from a hypodermic needle.

to seep into places in the brain where it doesn't belong. To make matters worse, damaged blood vessels and cells clog up the main blood flow to the brain. The result could be death. However, if meningitis is detected in time, it can be cured with strong medication such as antibiotics.

Meningitis is only one of many serious diseases carried in the bloodstream. Perhaps the most destructive disease that the blood encounters is septicemia, blood poisoning caused by bacteria. It occurs after another major disease, such as meningitis, has destroyed organs in the body. The bacteria are still alive and look for someplace else to continue growing. That place is the blood. The bacteria invade the bloodstream and start attacking the blood just as they did the rest of the body. The blood starts clotting inside the blood vessels. This restricts the flow of blood to places such as the kidneys and brain. After that, the body shuts down and dies.

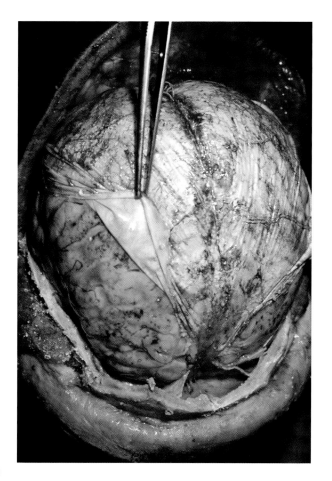

Meningitis is so dangerous because it breaks through the blood-brain barrier and allows blood and bacteria to seep into the brain. Here you can see how the blood has passed through the meninges.

Many viruses and bacteria produced by nature can destroy the human body. Some of them can be quite ghastly. A rare disease caused by the Ebola virus leads to death by dissolving blood vessels, causing patients to bleed internally and uncontrollably. The disease is found only in Africa, and it is almost always fatal. Researchers have no idea where it comes from or how to stop it. Many other viruses that travel in the blood, such as HIV, cannot be cured. They are just too strong, and too complicated, for science to figure out how to stop them. Yet.

Some diseases that affect the blood have nothing to do with outside forces such as microorganisms. Diabetes, for example, occurs when the body cannot manage the level of sugar, or glucose, in the blood. Glucose is converted to fuel for our cells, and it needs to remain at a consistent level to keep cells working properly. When the body mismanages glucose, it causes diabetes. Diabetic blood is too full of sugar, which clogs it up and prevents it from doing its job properly. Diabetes sometimes has to be treated with a medicine called insulin to bring the sugar levels back to normal. Untreated, it can cause heart disease and strokes.

Many people with diabetes are born with it, but it can also affect people who are overweight or have poor eating habits. Diabetes is a huge health concern in America and Europe, as a poor diet and obesity have caused more people to become diabetic. Nearly 10 percent of all Americans have diabetes, and for people over the age of sixty, the percentage is almost 25.

Overall, blood is good at handling the most common diseases (meningitis, Ebola, anthrax, and AIDS are all extremely serious, but relatively rare). In fact, many of the diseases in your body happen when your blood is unable to do its job properly. Heart disease, the number-one killer in the United States, occurs because your arteries become clogged by a buildup of something called plaque. This prevents oxygenated blood from getting to your heart.

Plaque is a hard substance that builds up on the walls of arteries (it is different from the plaque on your teeth, even though it has the same name). The plaque in your blood vessels is caused by minute damage to the artery walls. White cells build up around this damage and then attract fatty substances, which harden over time and eventually block the flow of blood. Plaque can also break off in chunks and clog the heart and its valves, leading to a heart attack. This can cause your heart to stop, a condition called cardiac arrest.

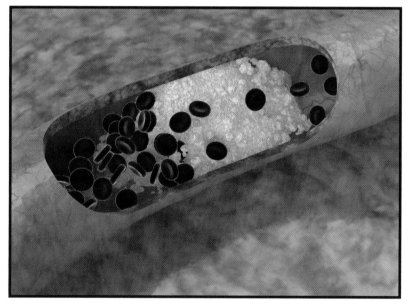

When a similar blood blockage occurs in the brain, it is called a stroke. This commonly affects older people. Plaque clogs the arteries leading into the brain, limiting the necessary blood supply. The result is a stroke, which injures the part of the brain that isn't getting enough blood. Stroke victims often experience some paralysis and loss of speech. The arteries in the stroke area can often be cleared with medicine, and many people are able to recover fully if treated properly and in time.

Of course, the worst thing that can happen to the body's blood supply is to lose it. Major injuries, such as those from a car

Plaque buildup in your blood vessels prevents a steady flow of blood, which can cause strokes and heart attacks.

crash or a gunshot in battle, can cause blood to flow freely out of a wound. When the body loses a lot of blood, the amount of blood flowing through the heart is reduced. This dramatically lowers the pressure of the blood. Lower blood pressure means that less blood is pumped into places such as the brain, which needs a certain amount of blood—and its oxygen—to function properly. If the brain, or any other organ, doesn't get enough oxygen, it starts failing. This major loss of blood is called shock.

You might have heard on the news that an accident victim "went into shock." Most people think this means "shocked," as if the victim couldn't believe the horrible thing he or she had just gone through and it was affecting their emotions. This is completely wrong. Medical shock refers to a blood pressure so low that it affects the operation of the organs. Emotional shock is the way people feel or think after experiencing an extremely disturbing event. It's a big difference, and medical shock can be fatal.

Severe accidents can also cause internal bleeding. This occurs if, for instance, an organ is ruptured in a fall or if the body crashes into something. Internal bleeding results from severed blood vessels. An organ that is bleeding is said to be hemorrhaging. This means that blood is flowing out of the circulatory system, but the word is most often used to describe bleeding inside the body. Such bleeding must be treated immediately by a doctor. A hemorrhage can result in low blood pressure. It can also damage organs and tissue because the free-flowing blood interrupts their normal operation.

A hemorrhage occurs in instances such as a brain aneurysm. An aneurysm is a swelling on the wall of a weak blood vessel, kind of like a bubble that you make with bubblegum. If this aneurysm occurs in a brain vessel and the vessel bursts, blood spills into the brain. Suddenly blood is going to places it shouldn't go instead of through the proper channels. If not treated immediately, a person who experiences an aneurysm can die because the body has no way to repair the broken blood vessel.

In the cases of people who lose a lot of blood, the body cannot produce enough of its own blood to make up for the loss.

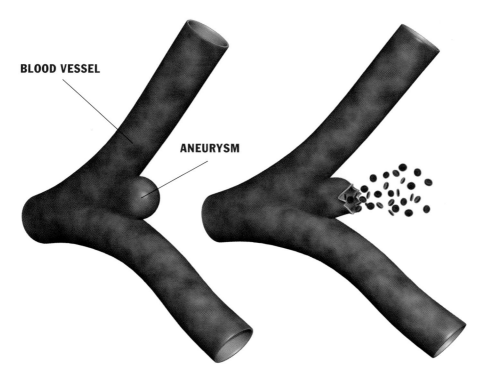

This is also true for patients who undergo major surgery, such as heart operations or organ removal. The only way to treat extreme blood loss is to provide patients with blood via a transfusion. Fortunately, transfusions help to save thousands of people every day.

Keeping your blood healthy, and inside you, is vital to you every moment of your life. All animals need healthy blood in order to survive. But some animals have stranger blood than others.

An aneurysm is like a bursting bubble in the brain.

Red Blood, Blue Blood, Clear Blood, Cold Blood

The way our blood works in our bodies makes sense to us. It flows from the heart to the other organs. It turns red when it picks up oxygen from our lungs. It travels through arteries and veins and capillaries. It serves as a means to deliver fuel to our cells and remove waste from our bodies. In all, it's an extraordinarily efficient system for keeping us alive.

What works for humans, though, doesn't necessarily work for other creatures. In fact, there are some creatures whose blood systems are so bizarre, they seem as if they would be more suited to life on another planet.

Start with the simple cockroach. One of the most common insects on earth, the cockroach can survive for weeks after having its head cut off. The reason? It has an open circulatory system, which means that its blood sloshes around inside its body as if it was inside a jar. Once the cockroach loses its head, this blood immediately clots around the wound in a thick liquid, which creates a plug in its neck. If the cockroach had blood vessels like those of humans, the blood would pour out as if from a fire hose. It also helps that cockroaches are cold-blooded, which means they don't have to eat as much as warm-blooded mammals. This is a benefit, since their eating apparatus disappears with their heads.

Many animals on the planet, with the obvious exception of mammals and birds, are cold-blooded. This includes reptiles, fish, amphibians, arachnids, and insects. Actually, their blood isn't really cold like ice water or snow. "Cold-blooded" is a term for animals that are ectotherms. This means they can't regulate their internal body temperature; instead they take on the temperature of their surroundings. That's why lizards and snakes like to bask on rocks in the sun; it keeps their bodies warm. The heat from the sun is converted to energy and helps them hunt for prey and digest their food. When it's too cold, though, ectotherms have a hard time moving around; cold weather makes them sluggish.

Yet, cold-blooded creatures can typically live on less food than

A cockroach can live without its head for weeks due to the way its blood clots in its neck.

warm-blooded creatures of the same size. Warm-blooded animals require more food because they need the fuel to keep themselves warm. Ectotherms adapt to whatever the outside temperature is.

Interestingly, bats—one of the mammals we often associate with the scarier side of blood—are unable to regulate their internal temperature. They cool off only when they are at rest. This makes them almost a cross between warm- and cold-blooded creatures.

We use the term "cold-blooded" to refer to particularly nasty

or evil people because we associate that nastiness with snakes, alligators, and lizards. These animals aren't nasty, and they're not truly cold-blooded, but the term lives on.

There is one animal that we could classify as being truly cold-blooded. It's the mackerel icefish, and it lives in the frigid waters surrounding Antarctica. The icefish, which looks like a misshapen crocodile, is the only known animal with a backbone (a vertebrate) that doesn't have hemoglobin in its blood. Instead, the blood of the icefish is made up of a clear kind of antifreeze that keeps ice

By soaking up the sunshine on a warm rock, this lizard is heating its entire body—something it cannot do by itself.

crystals from forming inside its body. It is believed that since the icefish has no hemoglobin, it absorbs oxygen through its skin.

While the icefish's blood is ideally suited to helping it survive in temperatures that drop below freezing, another creature uses its blood to survive attacks by enemies. This is the horned lizard. Found across North America, it is often called the horny toad, but in reality it is a very odd lizard with a unique skill. When the horned lizard is attacked by a predator—such as a coyote or a fox—it squirts blood out of its eyeballs into the face and mouth of the attacker. The streams of blood can reach up to five feet. The horned lizard accomplishes this feat by increasing the blood pressure in the front of its head, which results in blood bursting through the vessels of the eyes. Apparently its blood has a hideous taste that sends predators running in the other direction. The lizard isn't harmed by this effort, although it looks gruesome

The icefish has clear blood that serves as an antifreeze keeping ice crystals from building up in its body.

The horned lizard is one of a few creatures that use their blood as a defensive weapon.

OTHER KINDS AND COLORS OF BLOOD

lood has three primary colors in the animal kingdom. Not surprisingly, they are red, blue, and yellow. Most land animals have red blood due to the presence of hemoglobin, a protein that turns red when it bonds with oxygen. The blood of many mollusks, such as squids, octopuses, and slugs, is blue because these creatures have hemocyanin proteins instead of hemoglobin. Hemocyanin turns blue when it is exposed to oxygen. Then there are sea squirts, which live deep in the ocean and spend their lives attached to a single piece of coral or rock. Their blood contains hemovanadin, which turns yellow when it is exposed to oxygen.

Human blood can turn green if a person suffers from sulfhemoglobinemia, a disease that occurs when hemoglobin absorbs atoms of sulfur instead of oxygen molecules. It is an extremely rare condition, but is so strange that it has been called alien blood by some observers.

with blood covering its face after the streaming stops.

We might find this process rather gross, but the horned lizard was revered by some ancient American cultures for its ability to "weep blood." They saw the positive side of the horned lizard's unique skill.

The strangest of all blood systems, though, has to belong to the horseshoe crab. This crab (which is not a crab at all but is closer in evolution to scorpions) has been around since before the age of the dinosaurs, and it has a huge shell that looks like a spiked helmet. One of the most fascinating things about the horseshoe crab is that it has blue blood. This is due to its having copper as a base for its blood instead of iron, which is the basic element in red-blooded creatures. Blue blood uses hemocyanin ("cyan" is another name for "blue") instead of hemoglobin to help it store oxygen.

The horseshoe crab's unusual blood isn't limited to its color. It has an open circulatory system, which means that its blue blood washes around inside its body without traveling through blood

The horseshoe crab's blood is not only blue but kills just about every kind of bacteria it touches.

vessels. But what makes the horseshoe crab's blood really incredible is that it can destroy some of the most potent bacteria on earth. When the crab's blood is exposed to even a single bacterium, it forms a clot around the bacterium and prevents it from moving into the crab's body.

Horseshoe-crab blood is so sensitive that pharmaceutical companies use it to test the purity of medicines that are to be injected into humans. Before the medicine is shipped to a local doctor or pharmacy, it is inserted into a sample of horseshoe-crab blood. If the crab blood clots, it means there are bacteria in the medicine, and it's not pure enough. Only when there is no clotting is the medicine ready to be used by people.

Horseshoe-crab blood is also the best way to determine the sterility of the instruments that are used during surgery. This is especially important when doctors operate on patients with

Medical technicians extracting blue blood from horseshoe crabs in a laboratory.

infectious diseases. Testing the equipment used in the surgical suite with a solution containing horseshoe-crab blood ensures that everything is as sterile as possible. There is no other chemical, material, or test that can detect bacteria as well as the blue blood of a horseshoe crab. Scientists are trying to find a way to synthesize horseshoe-crab blood so that they won't have to remove blood from living crabs.

Most animals have fairly normal blood systems—at least by human standards—which makes these creatures so unusual. But there is another group of creatures whose relationship to blood is altogether spooky. That's because they need human blood to help them survive. You know what they are: mosquitoes, leeches . . . and vampires.

115

CHAPTER 9

The Creeps

We like the thought of our blood staying right where it is—safe and sound inside our bodies. We certainly don't like the idea that something else might want to take our blood away from us.

But some creatures do want human blood. Some of them fly, some crawl, and others slither. They often attack in the dark, and they are usually so silent, we never hear them coming. The one thing they have in common is that they have to puncture our flesh to get at our blood.

Blood is their food.

Creatures that drink blood are known as hematophagous animals ("hema" comes from the Greek word for "blood"). Despite their sinister habits, they are usually harmless, and we're not even aware that they've bitten us until they've finished the job and moved on. But sometimes their bites can kill.

The deadliest hematophagous animal is a creature you've seen hundreds of times. The mosquito.

The mosquito is the most common bloodsucker in the world. There are more than three thousand species of mosquito, and they are found on every continent with the exception of Antarctica. The mosquito (its name means "little fly" in Spanish) is not only an annoying pest but also the world's single deadliest creature.

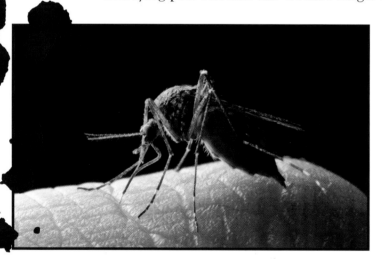

Only the female mosquito drinks blood. Males never do. This is because the female needs the sugar from blood to help her generate and nourish her eggs. After she has laid her eggs, the female can live on juice from fruit and other plants. But as soon as she is ready to produce more eggs, she needs blood.

The mosquito finds you by using a complex system of heat sensors and carbon dioxide detectors. She can follow the carbon dioxide you exhale, and then use her heat sensors to locate the right spot on your skin. Color may also play a role in helping the mosquito zero in on the right target. No one is sure exactly why, but mosquitoes are attracted to very dark colors, such black and navy

Female mosquitoes drink human blood in order to provide nourishment for their larvae.

blue. This could be due to the fact that these colors absorb heat (light colors would reflect heat) or that they stand out from the greens, browns, yellows, and other colors that are more prevalent in nature.

Once she lands on your flesh—so gently that you rarely feel it—the female goes to work. The proboscis, or pointed mouthpart, of a mosquito is designed like a hypodermic needle, which is the device doctors use to inject or extract blood from you during medical examinations. The mosquito uses this needlelike mouth to pierce your skin and drill into a capillary.

The incredible part of this process is not the sharp mouth, but the saliva. A mosquito's saliva contains an anesthetic that keeps you from feeling her mouth puncture your skin. It also contains an anticoagulant that keeps blood from clotting while she is sucking the blood out. This way, she can suck quickly without the blood's getting clogged by platelets. (Scientists have begun studying the chemical makeup of mosquito saliva to try to develop similar anesthetics and anticoagulants.)

The mosquito sucks as much blood from a capillary as she can, then pulls out and flies away. It is only after the anesthetic wears off that you feel the bite, and by that time your body is already reacting to it. Seeking to fight off the effect of the saliva, your skin creates the bump that we all know as a mosquito bite.

The mosquito takes so little of your blood that your body never notices it's gone. What makes the mosquito dangerous is that she goes from person to person and pierces him or her with her mouth—which brings the blood from one person into contact with that of another. This means that if the mosquito drinks the blood from someone with a disease caused by certain parasites, she can transmit them to the next person she bites through her saliva. This is like getting a disease by injecting tainted blood or using a dirty hypodermic needle.

Unfortunately, the mosquito can carry some of the deadliest diseases in the world. Although many of these diseases, such as malaria, are treatable and are rarely found in industrialized countries, they are especially deadly in parts of Africa, Asia, and South America. These places have too few doctors and too little medication to treat the people infected by mosquitoes.

MOSQUITO DISEASES

he mosquito can carry viruses and parasites that are disease carriers. These include malaria, which breaks down red blood cells and can block the flow of blood to the brain. It also carries the flavivirus, a nasty bug that is responsible for dengue fever (it causes internal bleeding), West Nile virus (which causes brain disease), yellow fever (which leads to vomiting of blood and coma), and eastern equine encephalomyelitis (which causes brain and spinal cord disease).

Mosquitoes don't transmit all diseases because not all viruses and parasites can survive the transmission process. For instance, the human immunodeficiency virus (HIV) that causes AIDS is actually digested and destroyed inside the mosquito.

Mosquitoes are known as a disease vector, meaning they do not cause the actual disease but transmit and spread the disease by carrying it from one host to another. Mosquitoes themselves are never affected by the diseases they carry.

A poster warning people of the danger of getting malaria from mosquitoes.

Every year, mosquitoes spread diseases that kill more than one million people—some health organizations think the number of deaths is closer to five million. If you add this number up every year, you'll quickly discover that mosquitoes have been responsible for billions of deaths over the course of human history. It is likely that this tiny insect has killed more humans than all other animals combined.

Like mosquitoes, most creatures that use human blood for food are insects. These include the bedbug (which has become an increasingly dangerous pest since the beginning of the twenty-first century, due in part to its resistance to pesticides), sand flies, horseflies, ticks, and fleas. Many of them also drink the blood of other mammals and don't limit their bloodsucking to people.

The strangest animal to feed on blood is the leech. A large sluglike creature about the size of a big thumb and resembling a hugely overgrown snail without its shell, the leech is found in numerous countries. There are many species of leeches, not all of which suck blood, but those that do are found in both water and on land. They attach themselves to swimmers or to people who are sleeping in leech-infested areas such as swamps.

Leeches latch on to you by using a long set of jaws that sink into your skin like a row of staples. Their saliva contains an anesthetic that minimizes—and sometimes completely prevents—any pain you might feel from the bite. Leeches also use a form of

Bedbugs bite . . . then drink your blood.

suction to hang on tightly to your skin. Once a leech is attached, it is very hard to remove it without hurting yourself. And the leech won't let go until it's finished getting what it wants.

Like the mosquito, the leech has anticoagulants in its saliva to keep your blood from clotting. This allows it a nice, constant supply of blood from the capillaries it has bitten into. Unlike the mosquito, though, the leech doesn't take a quick gulp and move on. It requires enough blood to fill its entire body, and can swell up to about five times its normal size to get extra blood. This amount can range anywhere from a teaspoon to a tablespoon or more. It's still not enough blood to affect your body, but it is incredibly gross and even frightening to think that this creature is locked onto your skin and drinking your blood.

Leeches drop off once they are completely full. They can also be pried loose by doctors or by gradually separating them from your skin a tiny bit at a time. Ripping them off quickly can be painful and can cause an infection.

In years past, sick people got to experience this bit of gruesomeness firsthand if they had doctors who believed in using leeches for bloodletting. Some doctors felt that leeches were

Leeches attach themselves to your skin and feed on your blood until they are full—then they drop off.

safer than lancets and easier to use for draining blood. They just attached a leech—or a few—let it do its work, and when the leech was finished, it popped off.

Though bloodletting never worked, surprisingly leeches turned out to be a good medical device. In just the last few years, leeches have been used to treat patients who'd undergone delicate surgery. In certain kinds of skin surgery—such as reattaching severed limbs—where there is a danger of capillaries' clotting up and preventing skin from healing, doctors put leeches on the area to speed up recovery. This happens thanks to the leeches' saliva.

The leech is placed on skin by doctors. It affixes itself to the wound, and its saliva, as well as its natural bloodsucking, keeps the blood flowing normally. This prevents clots and gives the body a chance to grow new capillaries that will connect across the gap in the skin. These particular leeches are grown in labs and used specifically for surgery. Doctors may require the use of several dozen of them to accomplish what modern medicine still cannot.

The leech may be repugnant, but the most frightening hematophagous creature is the vampire bat.

The vampire bat looks scarier than it really is and rarely harms its victims. The bat is made all the more frightening by the fact that it walks on the ground to get close to its victims, much like the "human" vampires in books and movies.

It is found primarily in Central and South America, and like all bats, it feeds at night. While most bats feast on fruit or insects, the vampire bat does indeed feed on blood. It will drink the blood of warm-blooded mammals, including cows, sheep, and humans.

Bats are well known for their ability to use radarlike signals to detect their prey. They send out high-pitched squeals that bounce off their insect prey and are received back in their ears. This is called echolocation. It allows bats to quickly find food even while flying in the dark. The vampire bat has a variation of this function, allowing it to also recognize the sounds of sleeping creatures, based primarily on their slow and shallow breathing. You can do this, too, as you can probably tell if a person is sleeping or awake by the way he or she breathes.

Once the bat has detected a sleeping human, it lands right near the body. Then it walks—yes, walks—over to the person and gently climbs up on him or her. Using a sensor in its nose, it finds a warm spot where blood is flowing just under the surface of the skin. This is often the carotid artery, which carries blood straight from the heart, up through the neck, and into the brain.

The vampire bat has two razor-sharp front teeth, which it quickly sinks into the victim, who rarely notices the bite. Like all hematophages, the vampire bat's saliva keeps the blood flowing once the puncture has been made (the vampire bat's saliva is called Draculin, but more on that in the next chapter). Instead of sucking the flowing blood, the bat licks it up with its tongue. It does this for about half an hour, usually taking an ounce or more of blood from its sleeping prey. Although the amount isn't enough to harm the prey, it's enough to actually double the entire weight of the vampire bat while it feeds.

When it is done, the bat walks away and then lurches into the air, flying back to join the hundreds of other bats that it lives with in a cave or tree. All that is left after it leaves its victim are the two puncture marks made by its fangs and a trickle of blood.

Vampire bats can occasionally transmit diseases such as rabies or cause infections in the people they bite. That they can drink blood and make people very ill—all without waking up their victims—makes them seem like silent demons. The thought of a vampire bat climbing up on you is enough to give you nightmares.

What if instead of a bat the vampire were actually a human? Someone who crept into your bedroom and sucked your blood while you slept? For many people, that might be the biggest nightmare of all.

CHAPTER 10

The Undead

One of the first horror movies ever made was called *Nosferatu*. It was produced in Germany and released in 1922. It told the story of Count Orlok, a creepy and scary-looking man who drank the blood of his victims in the dark of night. Orlok drank the blood of humans for one sinister reason: he was actually dead, and needed fresh blood so that he could still walk among the living. This made him "undead."

Since that time nearly a century ago, vampires and the undead have been featured in hundreds of movies made all over the world.

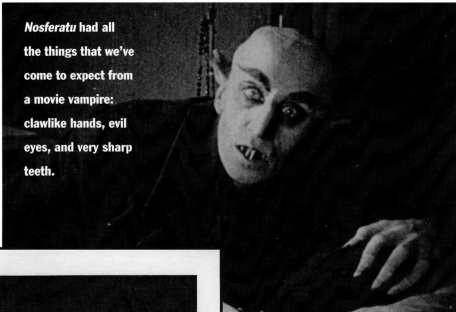

Nosferatu had all the things that we've come to expect from a movie vampire: clawlike hands, evil eyes, and very sharp teeth.

Bram Stoker 1906

Nosferatu is an adaptation of a book called *Dracula*, which was written in 1897 by an Irish novelist named Bram Stoker. *Dracula* is about a man from a mysterious place called Transylvania. His name is Count Dracula, and unbeknownst to those around him, he sleeps in a coffin during the day and sucks the blood of sleeping people during the night—just like a vampire bat.

Bram Stoker, the man who wrote *Dracula*, has inspired countless vampire stories over the last century.

Stoker's novel was based on the story of a prince named Vlad Tepes, a member of the royal family in what is now Romania, a country in eastern Europe. And the mysterious Transylvania is actually located in central Romania.

Vlad ruled during the mid-1400s. His family was part of the Order of the Dragon, called Dracul in his native language (the word derives from "Draco," the Latin word for "dragon"). Thus, he became known as Vlad Dracul.

Vlad was a particularly vile ruler. Many called him bloodthirsty. He thought nothing of having his enemies tortured

Vlad Dracul sits comfortably at a table, watching as his enemies are tortured and executed.

and murdered right in front of him. It is believed that he was responsible for tens of thousands of killings during his reign. One of his favorite methods of execution was to have a sharpened pole driven through the chests of his victims—a ghastly process called impaling—and then propping up the poles for all to see. For this he became known as Vlad the Impaler.

More than four hundred years later, Bram Stoker took some of the details of Vlad's life and used them as elements in his story: the name Dracul, the setting in Transylvania, and the use of sharp stakes through the chest. According to Stoker's story, the only way to kill a vampire was to drive a sharp stake through its heart.

Vlad, however, wasn't a vampire. He didn't actually drink his victims' blood. For that part of his book, Stoker used legends that had been told in Europe for centuries. Many cultures had stories of dead people who came out of graves to feed on the blood of the living. This enabled the undead to stay alive, if only at night. The horrific thing about the undead was that if you were bitten by one, you might become one of them.

These legends highlight people's fear of blood, and also its importance. After all, blood was considered powerful enough to help reanimate the dead. We know that blood was important in

The Transylvanian prince Vlad Tepes was one of the inspirations for the story of Dracula.

ancient rituals, and there were myths of gods who took blood from humans. The idea of people coming back from the dead to take blood from the living was particularly unusual, though. No one is sure exactly where these legends came from, but we do have a pretty good theory. And the legends go back to the plagues that ravaged Europe during the Dark and Middle Ages.

One of the symptoms of particular forms of the plague is bleeding from the mouth. Even though they had no medical knowledge, people of the time realized that this was a bad thing, and they ran away from those who bled. They knew these people had a disease and thought it might be a curse or a sign that bleeders were inhabited by the Devil. To keep from getting cursed themselves, they avoided these bleeders like . . . well, like the plague. Some of them were thought to be witches.

These were natural fears at the time, given the widespread lack of information, but by themselves they wouldn't have given rise to the notion of the undead. Even though sick people were bleeding, they were still very much alive. Something more threatening was at work.

A superstition arose that it wasn't just the living who might be cursed or possessed by the Devil. It was the dead, as well. Corpses came out of their graves and preyed on the living, drinking their blood at night when no one could see them. Maybe if they drank enough blood, these corpses could come back to "real" life. But where did such an extraordinary idea come from?

Researchers think they might have recently found the answer. In early 2009, the body of a woman was unearthed in Venice, Italy. She had died during a plague that had occurred in the 1500s in that city, and her body was in a mass grave. These graves are used during plagues or natural disasters when there is no time for proper

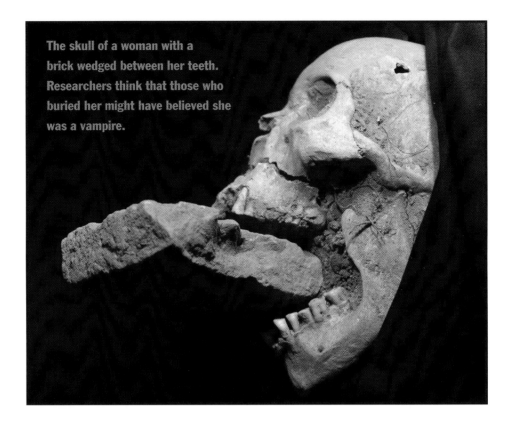

The skull of a woman with a brick wedged between her teeth. Researchers think that those who buried her might have believed she was a vampire.

burials because so many people die during such occurrences. The dead must be buried quickly before their bodies start to decay and possibly spread disease to those who are still alive.

What made the finding of this woman so bizarre was that she was found with a brick wedged into her mouth. But why?

The answer lay in other people who had been buried in mass graves. When people were buried, usually the only preparation was to wrap them in a large cloth called a shroud. This fit tightly around all parts of the body, especially the face and head. No other consideration, such as draining the body of its fluids or putting it in an individual coffin, was given. There was no time; too many other people had to be buried.

Without proper preparation, something strange—but

altogether natural—would happen to these bodies. They would swell from the gases still trapped in their organs. Some of their internal fluids, ranging from blood to bile, would be expelled from their mouths and noses (in the world of funerals and cemeteries, this is called purge fluid). This dark fluid would eat through the shroud like acid, leaving what looked like a bloody hole around the mouth.

In addition, the skin on the bodies would have shriveled up, revealing longer fingernails, more hair, and a very gaunt appearance. (This skin shrinking is the real reason that hair and fingernails appear to continue to grow after death; in fact, they do not.) It appeared as if the dead had continued to grow even after they had died.

During a plague, when the gravediggers returned to the mass grave to add new corpses, they were very likely to come across an unsettling sight. They would find that some of the older bodies appeared to have eaten through their shrouds and ingested blood. The gravediggers had never seen this actually happen; it must have occurred at night when they were asleep. Being superstitious, they believed that these "shroud eaters" had drunk blood in the dark of night and then returned to sleep in the grave so that no one would notice.

The discovery of the woman in Venice is evidence that people were worried about her coming back from the dead as a vampire. It is quite probable that the brick was used to prevent her from using her teeth to feed on the living when she emerged from the grave.

This finding helps establish the basis for much of the vampire legend, especially the parts about sleeping in graves and drinking blood from the living. But what about the notion that vampires must avoid sunlight? Some have tried to link it to a rare disease called porphyria. People born with this condition have difficulty producing hemoglobin properly, and thus have very pale skin and a sensitivity to bright sunlight. However, this is an extremely rare condition, and it is unlikely that there were enough sufferers to give rise to any legend.

This part of the vampire myth was probably created by storytellers because no one ever saw a vampire during the day. Plus, the real vampires—bats—came out only at night. Giving human vampires the ability to turn into bats was the last step in creating one of the world's most popular monsters.

Bram Stoker's *Dracula* was not the first vampire story, nor was it the last, but it certainly is the most famous. Over the last century, it has given rise to hundreds of movies, TV shows, Broadway musicals, and ever more books about vampires. It's truly amazing when you think of some of the popular characters that are based on Dracula and his vampire relatives: A series of black-and-white

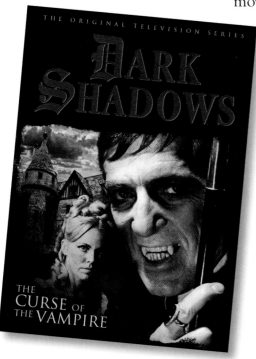

movies made in the 1930s starring Bela Lugosi as Count Dracula that are still popular to this day. The TV shows *Buffy the Vampire Slayer*, *True Blood*, and *Dark Shadows*. Anne Rice's novels about the vampire Lestat. The Count, *Sesame Street*'s devilish master of numbers. Count Chocula, the mascot of a breakfast cereal that bears his name. The blood-spitting bat character played by Gene Simmons of the rock group Kiss. The Underworld movies. Edward Cullen and his family in the Twilight series by Stephenie Meyer.

Dark Shadows was a popular daytime TV show in the 1960s.

It is probably no surprise to learn that the vampire, in some form or other, has appeared in more movies than any other fictional character in history. It ties in with our own uneasy feelings about blood—something that people all over the world share.

Video games, comic books, Halloween costumes, novels, theme-park attractions, and many other forms of popular entertainment all pay tribute to the bloodsucking ways of the vampire. These tributes are not all limited to entertainment; even the saliva of the vampire bat was named Draculin by scientists in honor of Bram Stoker's title character.

The image of the undead drinking blood is occasionally helped along by real-life figures. Notable among them was Elizabeth Báthory, a Hungarian countess who was born in 1560. Not long

Actor Bela Lugosi became famous for playing the character of Count Dracula, the vampire.

after her fiftieth birthday, Báthory was arrested and convicted for killing hundreds of young girls in her castle. No one is quite sure why she did this, but a legend arose that she bathed in the blood

of these girls to keep her skin healthy and help her live longer. In an interesting coincidence, her family ruled Transylvania for many years.

For centuries, the Maasai tribe of eastern Africa drank the blood of their cattle, usually mixed with milk, in order to add protein to their meals. They drink less of it today, as their diet has become more modern, but it is still an important part of their rituals such as celebrating a new birth. Though the Maasai never drank human blood, the idea that humans would drink any kind of blood is fascinating to most of the world.

There is no doubt that vampire legends will continue for as long as humans are around. Some authors, such as Richard Matheson in *I Am Legend*, have even speculated that the end of the world will ultimately be a showdown between vampires and regular people.

Countess Elizabeth Báthory was accused of bathing in the blood of young girls.

The Undead

All of this appeals to our interest in, as well as our fear of, blood. The more we learn about blood, though, the more we realize that it is nothing to be afraid of. That won't stop us from getting scared, or feeling squeamish, at the thought of a monster out there in the night that wants our blood. But even something as incredible as blood can't bring a human corpse back to life.

CHAPTER 11

Flowing, but Not Freely

Despite all we know about blood, the one thing we haven't figured out yet is how to make it. We can't make it in a lab or create it using chemicals. The only source of human blood is the human body.

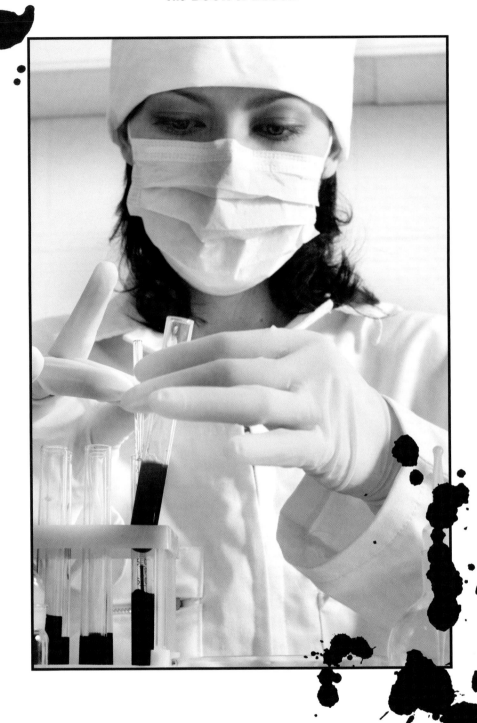

Blood cannot be made in a lab; it has to be
donated by people.

This makes blood one of the most valuable substances on the planet. A pint of blood that is sold to hospitals can cost more than $200. With eight pints to the gallon, that comes to more than $1,600 per gallon. By comparison, the price of a gallon of gas in the United States over the last few decades has ranged from $1 to $5.

The interesting thing is that the cost of gas reflects the money that oil companies have to spend drilling for it and refining it, along with transporting it to the gas station. Oil companies spend millions of dollars every year just trying to find new sources.

On the other hand, guess what the cost of getting blood is. Nothing. It's free.

In most countries blood is donated by volunteers. Several countries, such as China, pay for blood, but most, including

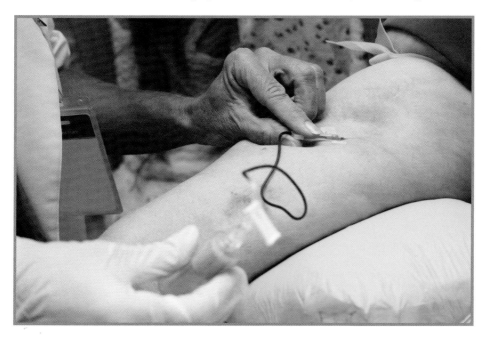

the United States, do not. They are concerned that people who desperately need money will give too much blood too often just for the money. There is also a feeling in many societies that blood

Donating blood doesn't hurt at all and helps save lives.

is a gift that should be given freely because a person wants to, not because he or she is making money from it.

Giving blood is a simple process that takes about fifteen minutes. It involves draining blood from a vein in your arm into an airtight plastic sack through a thin plastic tube. It is a relatively painless procedure, and about a pint is taken each time (donors have to wait several weeks before they can donate again, until the blood in their bodies is back to its normal quantity).

Donating blood is a noble and selfless act because the blood can be used to help those who need it. This can be almost anyone you can think of: a pregnant mom giving birth, an athlete injured while playing football, a soldier who is wounded during battle, a policeman who is suffering from a bullet wound, a fireman burned while putting out a house fire, a child being treated in the hospital for a serious disease, or a grandfather who is having his hip replaced.

American hospitals use about forty thousand units of blood every day.

RELIGION VERSUS BLOOD

Some religious groups, such as Jehovah's Witnesses, don't allow blood transfusions. It goes against their belief that "God will provide." This is based on a strict following of biblical rules such as this one from Acts 15:28–29: "For it seemed good to the Holy Spirit and to us to lay upon you no greater burden than these essentials: that you abstain from things sacrificed to idols and from blood." Many interpret this to mean that humans are not to take blood from any source, including potentially life-saving transfusions. These religious groups believe that should a patient die from blood loss, that simply means it is that person's turn to die, and this should be accepted.

People who do not want transfusions usually carry identification cards containing this information so that they are not accidentally given blood when they enter a hospital. When these individuals require surgery, doctors use special instruments to reduce blood loss during the operation.

Thus, even in modern times, there is still a strong belief in the religious significance of blood, and some people think of it as something sacred that should not be tampered with—no matter what the circumstances.

The number of blood donations typically increases in the aftermath of a disaster, such as the New Orleans floods caused by Hurricane Katrina in 2005 or the massive earthquake that occurred in Haiti in 2010. The reality, however, is that a huge amount of blood is needed all year round, not just during catastrophes. Hospitals in the United States use a combined total of nearly forty thousand pints of blood each and every day. Fortunately, donors give about fifteen million pints of blood a year, but there is always a need for more.

To keep a ready supply on hand, local hospitals and medical organizations called blood banks conduct blood drives, where they

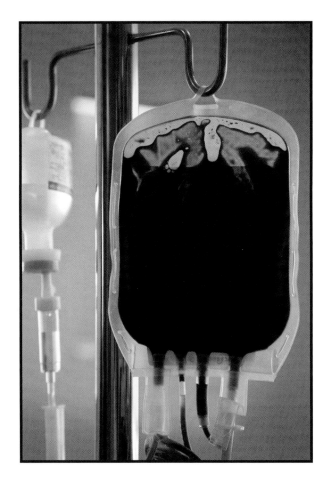

encourage people to come in and give a bit of their blood. Many adults regularly give to local blood banks, and they do it simply because this is a good thing to do and an easy way to help other people.

If blood is given for free, then how does it become so expensive by the time it gets to the hospital? The cost is due to all the steps that have to be taken in order to get the blood from a person's arm to the places that want to use the blood. It's not as simple as just forwarding the entire unit of blood from one place to another, because different parts of blood are used for different things. Many companies, laboratories, and medical facilities are involved in blood work, and they each charge a fee for their work.

After blood is collected, it is separated into its various parts using a centrifuge, which spins blood quickly. The blood easily divides into red blood cells, white blood cells with platelets, and plasma.

The RBCs are usually kept in local containers for use by hospitals, clinics, and paramedics. WBCs and platelets are used

144

Blood banks collect blood so that it can be processed and delivered to hospitals and laboratories.

to provide extra strength to the blood of patients undergoing surgery. This is especially important for people who are cancer and burn victims; they need extremely high levels of the defensive and clotting abilities of white blood cells and platelets.

Plasma is used for more things than RBCs and WBCs because of all the nutrients and chemicals it contains. Its clotting factors are needed for the treatment of hemophilia, its antibodies are used in the development of vaccines, and its albumin helps pharmaceutical companies create hormones and make various medicines more effective in the bloodstream.

Each of the blood components is broken down to its purest form, which can be liquid, semisolid, or even freeze-dried powder (similar to concentrated drinks like Kool-Aid or powdered lemonade). The blood parts then have to be tested to ascertain that they don't contain any diseases. During the 1980s, blood tainted with the virus that causes AIDS was accidentally given to hemophiliacs as part of their treatment

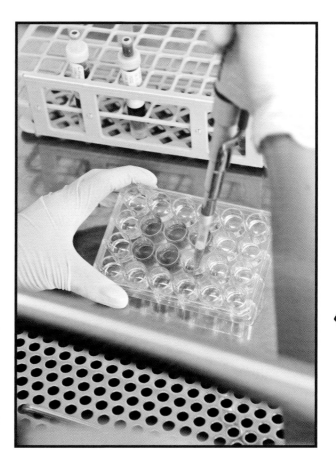

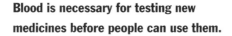
Blood is necessary for testing new medicines before people can use them.

for blood clotting, and more than half of these people contracted AIDS.

Since then, there has been extremely tight control over how blood is collected, treated, and transfused. It has to be processed in special machines, it has to be stored in special containers so that it won't be contaminated, and it has to be kept at the proper temperature so that it won't spoil.

All along the way, a dollar value is attached to blood because each stop requires that something be done to the blood, and each procedure costs money.

By the time blood comes back to a hospital for use during surgeries or emergency treatments, the patients are charged for it. This charge is a few hundred dollars per unit (or pint). A person undergoing heart surgery may need several dozen units during the course of an operation.

Hospitals are huge buyers of blood. So are research labs. Blood and its parts are critical to developing new medicines, and laboratories use blood to determine how it will react when it is exposed to different kinds of drugs.

Another big buyer is the government. Blood supplies have to be sent with the military into battle to treat wounded soldiers. To meet that potential demand, governments need to increase their collections before soldiers go into battle so that the blood will be ready right away.

Interestingly, warring nations can sometimes figure out when and where their enemies plan to fight by tracking their national blood drives. If a country is asking for more blood than usual, that means it might be getting ready for the injuries that always happen in battle.

Despite how much blood donors give, there is always the need for more. Every day in the United States, tens of thousands of units of blood are used to help people. They all need to be replaced in order to help the next group of patients. Because of this demand, there have been numerous attempts to create artificial blood. Unfortunately, none has been very successful. Blood is just too complex and performs too many functions for scientists to create something new that does everything it can do.

That leaves us wondering, what more can we learn about blood? Only in the last century have we learned that we have different blood types, how to transfuse it, and how it truly behaves in the body. One can only imagine what discoveries the next century holds.

Over the course of this book, you've learned a great deal about what blood is and what it isn't. You now know about hematophagous creatures and vampires and blood plasma and the circulatory system. Yet, you've just scratched the surface of all there is to know about blood. You'll find—as any good scientist will tell you—that the more you explore, the more fascinating things you'll uncover. And blood, which we all have, is one of the most fascinating and fabled substances in history.

Hopefully, the next time you see blood, you'll think of it as more than something red, scary, or gross. Perhaps you'll see it as the red fluid that fills up each and every person on the planet . . . and keeps all of us alive.

BIBLIOGRAPHY

BOOKS

In Search of Dracula: A True History of Dracula and Vampire Legends
By Raymond T. McNally and Radu Florescu
New English Library Ltd., published 1975

Bloodletting Instruments in the National Museum of History and Technology
By Audrey Davis and Toby Appel
Gutenberg e-book #33102, published 2010
www.gutenberg.org/files/33102/33102-h/33102-h.htm

Blood Rites: Origins and History of the Passions of War
By Barbara Ehrenreich
Holt Paperbacks, published 1998

Blood: An Epic History of Medicine and Commerce
By Douglas Starr
Knopf, published 1998

Blood Groups and Red Cell Antigens
By Laura Dean
Published by National Center for Biotechnology Information (NCBI), National Library
of Medicine, and National Institutes
of Health, 2005
www.ncbi.nlm.nih.gov/books/NBK2263

WEBSITES

The Merck Manuals Online Medical Library
Merck Sharp & Dohme Corp., published 2010
www.merckmanuals.com/home/index.html

Red Gold
Created by PBS/WNET 11
www.pbs.org/wnet/redgold/index.html

The Human Heart: An Online Exploration from
the Franklin Institute
www.fi.edu/learn/heart/blood/blood.html

Animation of Human Heart Beating
National Heart Lung and Blood Institute
www.nhlbi.nih.gov/health/dci/Diseases/hhw/hhw_pumping.html

Blood Groups, Blood Types, and Blood Transfusions
Presented by the Nobel Prize Organization
nobelprize.org/educational/medicine/landsteiner/readmore.html

Antique Bloodletting & Leeching Instruments
Medical Antiques.com
Created by Douglas Arbittier
medicalantiques.com/medical/Scarifications_and_Bleeder_Medical_Antiques.htm

PHOTO CREDITS

British Library: p. 16
Ethnologisches Museum Dahlem Berlin: p. 19
David Roberts: p. 35
The Franklin D. Roosevelt Library: p. 60
National Aeronautics and Space Administration (NASA): p. 72
Centers for Disease Control and Prevention: pp. 101, 121
Alfred Wegener Institute for Polar and Marine Research: p. 110
      (photo by Julian Gutt)
Associates of Cape Cod, Inc.: p. 113
Matteo Borini: p. 132
Dan Curtis Productions, Inc./MPI home Video: p. 134

ACKNOWLEDGMENTS

It is said that no book is ever created without a great deal of blood, sweat, and tears. For this book, there was more blood than usual, but it was pretty much confined to the words on these pages. However, there were a lot of people whose work turned my words into, as they say, a real "flesh and blood" book. They include Ken Wright, my fearless (and not at all bloodthirsty) agent; Kate O'Sullivan, my editor at HMH, whose guiding hand made this book a bloody good read; and the entire team at HMH, who went through much bloodletting to create the pages you have in front of you.

I want to thank my parents, for all of the blood, sweat, and tears they've shed for me over the decades. Thanks also to my blood relatives and their families, especially my nieces and nephews, as well as my extended family—by blood and marriage—for their ongoing interest and support. A full pint of gratitude to those who have been my blood brothers over the years: Michael Johnson and family, Tucker Greco and family, Bill Brahos and family, Peter Fitzpatrick, Bill McGuinness, Jim Shinnick, Al Mowrer, Philip Chapnick, and David Hill. And to Pete Prown and Rich Maloof, with whom I've put blood on many pages, and drawn blood during many discussions.

And finally, the three women for whom I would gladly spill my own blood: Trini, Madeline, and Katherine.

INDEX

Page references set in italics refer to illustrations and/or captions.

INDEX